My Feet
Aren't Ugly

My Feet Aren't Ugly

A GIRL'S GUIDE TO LOVING HERSELF FROM THE INSIDE OUT

BY DEBRA BECK

REVISED EDITION

 BEAUFORT BOOKS ■ NEW YORK

The Library of Congress has cataloged the first edition as follows:
Beck, Debra.
My feet aren't ugly : A girl's guide to loving herself from
the inside out / Debra Beck ; illustrations by Maggie Anthony.—1st ed. p. cm.

ISBN-13: 978-0-8253-0542-9 (pbk.: alk. paper)
ISBN-10: 0-8253-0542-X (pbk.: alk. paper)

1. Self-esteem in adolescence. 2. Self-acceptance in adolescence.
3. Teenage girls—Psychology. I. Title.
BF724.3.S36B43 2007
158.10835—dc22
2006034638

Revised Third Edition ISBN: 9780825309373

Book design by Jane Perini
Published in the United States by Beaufort Books, New York
www.beaufortbooks.com
Distributed by Midpoint Trade Books, a division of Independent Publishers Group
www.ipgbook.com

Printed in the United States of America

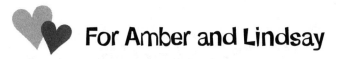 For Amber and Lindsay

Contents

ELEVEN

Have You Started Healing Yet?

 # Acknowledgments

This book would not have come to fruition if it weren't for the years I spent as a young mother growing up with my own two wonderfully spirited daughters, Amber and Lindsay. I thank them for being who they are and supporting me through this process in my life.

I am also grateful for all of the kids who inhabited my home during their teenage years, Nyla, Julie, Kim, Eric, Shelly, and Sharon to name a few. They gave me insight into my purpose in life.

I have so much gratitude for Maggie Anthony, my illustrator, for bringing life to my book and adding such a warm energy to the characters.

A special thanks goes out to Beaufort Books for making this book a reality and to Eric Kampmann for many laughs along the way. Many thanks to my book designer and good friend, Jane Perini, for the amazing cover and interior design that brings fun and love into my book in a way that I knew was possible. Finally, I am so deeply thankful for all the many mentors throughout my journey who have shared their wisdom and guidance so that I could be there for myself and these young girls in a whole different way.

My Feet Aren't Ugly

I hope *My Feet Aren't Ugly* will give you the seeds you need

to start planting a happy and empowered life for yourself.

–Debra

Introduction

As the alarm screamed, I threw my feet onto the floor and stretched with excitement because today was the first day of Spirit Week for Homecoming. The energy at school would be high, building up to the big night of Homecoming. I started to brush my teeth, my blurry eyes focused on my face in the mirror. Was that what I thought it was? Yep! It was — a pimple that seemed to be the size of a small grapefruit. I couldn't believe it. What was I going to do? All of the excitement from just moments before got rolled up into a ball, and it felt as if someone punched it into my stomach.

When I was a teenager, I was not so self-assured. I looked at my friends and the other girls, who all seemed to be so happy and confident, and I wondered what was wrong with me. I felt insecure and dumb. I thought I was an ugly, awkward, not-so-talented teenager. All the other girls in my class acted like they had it together: their hair was always perfect, their skin was clear, they looked like they came right out of the Abercrombie & Fitch catalog. I knew that getting ready for school could not be as challenging for them as it was for me.

Almost every morning when I looked at the clothes in my closet, I began to sweat. What was I going to wear? I began putting clothes on and pulling them off like I was a runway model. I'll wear my blue skirt with buttons down the front, with a white blouse. "Oh my God, no, no, no!" I looked like I worked at McDonald's. Okay, my green dress that everyone seemed to love. Suddenly, that didn't look right either. In fact, the floor was littered with clothes that didn't look right. What was I going to do? To make matters worse, not only was I sweating terribly, my hair was now poking up in some areas and sticking to my head in others. On mornings like this, I could feel a big knot in my stomach and tears welling up. When I finally settled on something to wear, like a pair of khaki shorts and a plain T-shirt, I'd look in the mirror, do a couple of turns, and think, "You must be kidding! This is your choice! This looks like something your mother picked out." (No offense, Mom.)

My insecurities didn't disappear. I took them with me through the better part of my young adulthood. I didn't figure out how to love myself until I was in my thirties. I decided to write this book not only for my own two young, spirited daughters, but to help other young girls learn how to love themselves and come into womanhood with a better sense of self. I don't want any teenage girl to go through what I went through before I learned to love myself.

Throughout the book there will be places where you can journal, to write down thoughts and actions and how they made you feel. Journaling is a way of expressing your feelings in a safe place, because no one is going to read it or judge it. It is a way to get to know yourself better and to gain clarity about issues you may be confused about. Another part I want you to pay extra special attention to is "A Teen's Journey." It highlights teens' comments about how they feel regarding the particular subject we are discussing. They share their experiences and lessons learned throughout their teenage years.

I hope when you read this book you take it to a quiet place, a place that allows your mind to really think about what is being said and how it applies to you. Most importantly, I just want you to have fun and enjoy it. I believe if you open your mind, you will get a lot out of it. So let's get this show on the road!

CHAPTER
ONE

Let's Learn to Like Ourselves

 So you want to be yourself and still be liked. Is this possible? What if you really liked yourself and if others liked you, great, but if they didn't, that would be okay too? Wouldn't it be a nice feeling not to care if everyone liked you? The way to do this is to develop SELF-ESTEEM.

The *Webster's Dictionary* description of self-esteem is having confidence and satisfaction in oneself. Let's take a look at what this really means.

A lot of people don't feel confident and satisfied with themselves. How do you feel? Liking yourself gives you self-esteem. *Do you like yourself? Are you likable?* When you like yourself, it gives you confidence and satisfaction. So, let's figure out how to like yourself.

First of all, it's hard to like yourself if you are not likable. I don't mean likable to other people as much as I mean likable to you. If you don't like yourself, it equals LOW SELF-ESTEEM. Don't try to fake being likable. There are few things worse than a fake "nice person." Everyone will see through your phoniness, including you.

Have you ever done things to yourself and other people that you don't feel good about? If you have, it is difficult to like yourself. In order to really like yourself, it is important to first look at the things you might do that would make you NOT like yourself.

DO YOU TALK BADLY ABOUT OTHERS OR TREAT PEOPLE POORLY?

Every time you make fun of someone or talk about people behind their backs, you act like you're better than they are. It leaves you feeling bad because you know deep down that you are not better than they are.

Human nature is good. You don't really want to hurt anyone. Saying mean things about people hurts you as much as it hurts them.

When I was thirteen years old, I went to school and it was one of those bad-hair days. I was already paranoid about the way I looked, and a guy in my math class told me my two girlfriends had told him that my hair looked like wet dog hair. I laughed — to act like it didn't hurt my feelings — but it did. I thought they were my friends. How could they say such a mean thing?

Do you know the old saying, "Do unto others as you would have them do unto you?" If we all lived our lives this way, we would be living in a much kinder world. Be aware of what you are saying and doing to everyone. Think to yourself, "If this were being said or done to me, would it feel bad?"

A Teen's Journey

I made fun of this girl in school who didn't seem very smart and found out that she had been in an accident and had brain surgery. It made me feel like a mean person and made me feel crummy about myself. It was a hard lesson. I still feel guilty about it.

Think it over... and Journal

On this page, write down everything you can think of that people do to you or others that makes you not like them. (Example: talking badly behind a friend's back, lying to save face, being snobby, acting like they are better than you.) Also write about how these things make you feel.

_____

_____

_____

_____

_____

_____

_____

_____

_____

_____

Now, look! Are any of these things you have done to others? If you are doing things that you don't like in others, how are you going to like yourself?

Think it over... and Journal

Now, write down the things you do to others that you don't like, and describe how you think it makes them feel, and how you feel.

_____

_____

_____

_____

_____

_____

_____

_____

_____

_____

Isn't it amazing how it makes you feel badly when you don't treat people right?

Work on these things daily to try and change your actions. If you are talking badly about people, STOP! Every time you find yourself talking about someone, stop and then say something nice about them instead.

MAKING DECISIONS IN LIFE AS IF
THEY AFFECTED EVERYONE

Sometimes we want something so badly that we take it no matter what, even if it hurts someone else. When I was fifteen years old, I liked this one guy very much, and I thought he liked me. We were actually hanging out a little. I had a few friends at my house one day, and my girlfriend, Kelly, started talking to him, and they left the group to be alone. I was very upset with Kelly because, again, I thought she was my friend and friends are supposed to care about each other. When I asked her about going off with him, she said it wasn't that big of a deal. Well, it was a big deal to *me*. Maybe not to her — she was on the side of the situation that was fun. I wasn't. She went with him without thinking about me, and she started liking him too. I think deep down Kelly felt bad about how she treated me, but her actions changed the relationship that we had. We weren't as close after that experience.

Doing things to get what you want without any regard for how your actions will affect others leaves you feeling badly about yourself. Have you ever done something that you knew would hurt or disappoint another person, and the one person most hurt or disappointed was you? We all want to be kind human beings. When we're not, we disappoint ourselves, which makes us dissatisfied with ourselves — which in turn gives us LOW SELF-ESTEEM.

Think it over. . . and Journal

What things have you done that have really hurt someone else and made you feel terrible? Write them down and tell how you felt and how you would have felt if those things had been done to you.

_____

_____

_____

_____

_____

_____

_____

_____

_____

Sometimes we don't even think about what we do to others or how they feel. That is why it is good to turn the tables around and put ourselves in their shoes to see how it would feel if it were us.

HAVING INTEGRITY

Integrity is having an uprightness of character or action. It implies trustworthiness. You know your code of honor; you know when you show a lack of integrity, in other words, when you are not trustworthy. It is very important to develop integrity within oneself. When you lie, cheat, steal, or deceive, you hurt yourself. You damage your self-esteem. You never want to do something that makes you view yourself as someone without integrity. *Isn't it hard to like people who lack integrity?* It can be difficult to be around those kinds of people, so make sure that you aren't one of them. Remember what the goal is — to like yourself. This sounds simple, but it isn't that easy.

Let's look at something as simple as copying someone's homework. Deep down you know this is wrong. In ninth grade when I copied a friend's homework, I can't even tell you how I felt while I copied it and after I turned it in. I was so nervous; my stomach felt like the swimming team was inside there doing laps. Then my teacher came up to me and said, "Debra, what a great job on your homework!" At first I felt relieved that she hadn't caught me, but then I just got even sicker inside. I thought I was going to throw up right there in front of the entire class. I felt like a cheater, and for a good reason: *I WAS A CHEATER.*

I felt bad about myself for days; I knew I had hurt my self-esteem.

Your goal here is simple: it is to like yourself. You must be careful and really think about the things you do. We all know the basics: not to lie, cheat, or steal. We are taught this at a very early age. But sometimes we forget the reasons why we shouldn't lie, cheat, or steal. Doing any one of these things makes us feel terrible inside. Doing any of these things

doesn't make it easy to like ourselves. Our parents told us not to do these things because they were bad. It's time to understand why.

Lying is another example of not having integrity. My daughter told me a story about a time she stayed home from school sick, only to go to the other side of town to hang out with a friend of hers. She said that she was so nervous and scared that she actually made herself sick to her stomach. When they tried to get on the bus to come home, my daughter and her friend got picked up by the police for skipping school. She was busted! She said it was impossible to have a good time because she was so worried.

When I was younger, I told my mother I was spending the night at a friend's. Instead a bunch of us went to a park and stayed out all night. When my mom asked me about what we did and I lied, I felt horrible. When you lie it affects you on a physical level, you actually feel it in your body. If you find yourself telling a lie, STOP! Work on changing the things you dislike in others in yourself first. If you do, you're on your way to higher SELF-ESTEEM.

A Teen's Journey

Integrity means to me that you're honest with not only the people around you but also with yourself. Whenever I am not being honest, I feel it in my stomach. This is the best way for me to tell because sometimes I'm not aware of my actions.

I was talking with a young girl named Kristy. She said she told this guy she liked that her parents let her drink whenever she wanted and as much as she wanted. I asked her if her parents allowed this behavior, and she said no. I asked her why she lied to him. She said because she wanted him to think she was cool. I asked her if she wanted a boyfriend who thought drinking was cool. She said, "No way." I then asked her if she was happy about who she was. She said not really, that she didn't like herself most of the time.

Lying does a lot of things to you. First it gives you an unsettled feeling because you get confused about who you really are. You might even start believing your lies. Second, it takes options away from the person you are lying to. Now this boy thinks he is dating a certain person who is allowed to drink whenever and as much as she wants. The reality is, he isn't. He isn't dating an honest person. If you liked yourself, you wouldn't have the need to lie. If Kristy thought she was okay the way she was, she wouldn't need this guy to think she was cool. Also she would start to attract guys that she was actually compatible with. If she doesn't drink and this guy likes her because he thinks she does, what kind of a relationship is that going to be? Lying hurts us in many different ways, and it hurts the person we are lying to as well.

Take stealing. When we take something that belongs to someone else, it violates that person. We do harm to him or her and fail to show the proper respect each human being deserves. Again, turn the tables on yourself. What if you had a special necklace that your grandfather gave you? How would you feel if someone took it? I myself would feel angry — angry with the horrible person who stole it. And sad — sad about not having it anymore. Sad that there are people in the world doing such unkind things. Remember, you have to think clearly about the things you do, because you play a really important part in the world. You affect everyone in it.

Every time we do something to someone, good or bad, it affects them. When you say something nice about someone or do something positive, they feel good about themselves. When you do the opposite to someone, that person has their feelings hurt. When they go home very unhappy, their unhappiness makes the people they live with feel unhappy too.

It's the ripple effect. Everything we do affects people, a lot of people, sometimes people we don't even know. It is important for you to do your best not to hurt people. We can choose to play a positive role in the world or a negative one. *Which do you choose?*

Here's a good example of what I am talking about. Remember the story earlier about my friends saying my hair looked like a wet dog? I felt crummy all day. When I was around other friends my bad mood put them in a bad mood. When I went home after school I remember treating my sister badly and she got in a bad mood. It actually affected our whole family.

Think it over... and Journal

Pay attention and write about the things you have said and done to others and how it affected them (positive things as well as negative things). Write down examples of what people's reactions were. Write about how you felt and how their reactions made you feel.

_____

_____

_____

_____

_____

_____

_____

_____

_____

Check in with yourself. When you do something that is negative, isn't it weird how it makes you feel sad? Also look at the reverse. Doesn't it feel great when you do something nice that spreads positive energy?

FINISHING PROJECTS

Another thing we might do that would hurt our self-esteem would be something as simple as starting a project and not completing it.

It's like starting a race and not finishing — dropping out. It makes you feel like you lost. You see yourself as a loser. You don't want to do anything that makes you feel like a loser. You want to be a winner in your own eyes, and you always want to finish the race. Finishing the race doesn't mean being first, it simply means that if you start the race, you finish it.

It is the same with any project. When you start a project and finish it, it gives you a sense of accomplishment. You're proud of yourself. Even with homework, when you don't finish what you start, it leaves you feeling badly about yourself. Guess what this does? Right! It gives you low self-esteem.

Two of my friend's daughters, Lauren and Maya, were staying with me. At about 5:30 p.m., we decided to go out and grab a bite to eat. Then Lauren said she had an assignment that needed to be done before a field trip the next day. I suggested she not go to dinner with us. We would bring her food back, so that she could get it done. She said that was a good idea. Then she showed up at the restaurant saying she didn't know where to begin.

Sometimes when we put our projects off until the last minute we become so overwhelmed we really don't know where to begin. So Lauren ate with us, and then we all went back to my house. She told us that she really needed our help, that there was no way she was going to be able to finish it by tomorrow without our help, and there was no way she could just not do it. We spent the next two hours helping her, and the project got finished.

Later, I asked her how it made her feel being under all that pressure and also maybe not doing the job up to her standards. She said that it made her feel like "crap." She had been nervous about it all day and the tension just kept building. Then she was anxious the next day because she wasn't sure how the others on her team would feel about the work she had done. The good thing was that she finished the project, no matter what. The bad thing was not leaving enough time to enable her to do the assignment up to her own standards.

Another good story about completing projects is from Caitlin, a fifteen-year-old who started an extracurricular photography class. She needed to complete a particular photography project so that her photos could be exhibited in an upcoming show. For some

reason Caitlin wasn't taking the assignment that seriously, and she waited until the last minute, then realized there was no way she was going to be able to finish. So she told the teacher that she had a lot going on and that she didn't have any of her photographs ready for the show. The teacher was very disappointed. So was Caitlin. She felt like such a loser. She said she even told herself she was a loser. She missed out on such a wonderful opportunity, although the lesson learned was great. She realized that when she doesn't finish a project, she views herself in a negative way. Once she let herself down by not following through, Caitlin would "bad-talk" herself and start to question her capabilities. She then realized how important it was for her to first, finish her projects, and second, make sure she gave herself enough time to do a good job.

You always want to hold yourself in high esteem. It is critical to do things in our lives that make us feel good about ourselves. So if it's an assignment with a due date, don't leave it to the last minute; make sure you have the time and energy to finish it on time and be able to give it your all.

Think it over. . . and Journal

Make a list of all the things that you have accomplished, and how they made you feel when you finished them.

_____

_____

_____

_____

_____

_____

_____

_____

_____

_____

_____

_____

WOW! Isn't that great? Aren't you proud of yourself?

WHAT IF YOU DON'T EAT RIGHT OR EXERCISE?

When you don't take care of yourself inside and out, it makes you feel bad. When you feel bad on the outside, your insides are also being damaged. When your eating habits affect the way you look, you say things to yourself that might not be good for you to hear — *especially* coming from yourself.

Have you ever made comments to yourself like, "Hey, Fatty, go ahead and eat another donut. Your pants aren't tight enough yet"? Every time we think negative things about ourselves, we believe them. If I tell myself I'm fat, guess what? I believe it. Our subconscious mind doesn't question what we tell it. Your subconscious is that place in your mind from which memories, feelings, or thoughts can influence your behavior without you realizing it. Your mind is very powerful, so be careful. You don't want to make it enemy territory!

We believe what we tell ourselves, so let's say positive things to ourselves. Instead of saying to yourself, "Hey Fatty, eat another donut," a better thing to say to yourself might be, "I am watching my weight so I can drop a few pounds and feel healthier." And then don't eat the second or third donut.

So the best thing to do is check in with yourself. It's probably *not* okay to eat five donuts, but one donut might be all right. You intuitively know how many donuts you can eat before it feels like you've overdone it. If you eat a donut, don't "bad-talk" yourself. Enjoy it. However, if you find that you're eating too many donuts, sit down and have a talk with yourself. Put yourself on an eating schedule that will make you feel good. If you're confused about how to eat properly, talk to a P.E. teacher, nurse, counselor, or someone at home. Go online and find information on nutrition, and find out how to eat healthily.

Here's a great website on some simple nutritional facts: girlshealth.gov Be sure to check out the nutrition and fitness sections.

Eating healthy and always enough of the right foods to nourish your body and soul is very important. Talk to your parents about bringing healthier foods into the house and starting to eat healthier as a family. I loved it when I learned to eat healthy foods, and found that I could eat a lot more food than I thought and still feel good physically. When I feel good physically, I feel good about myself.

A healthy diet shows how much you care about yourself; it is a reflection of how you feel about yourself. I always try to eat the right things although I'm not perfect.

BEING IN FRIENDSHIPS WITH PEOPLE WHO TREAT YOU RIGHT

When you allow people to treat you poorly, it's because you don't feel worthy of being treated with respect. Poor treatment can be as simple as a friend saying she will do something with you and not showing up or calling to let you know her plans have changed. It could also be her talking about you behind your back. You know in your inner core when one of your friends is treating you badly. Try not to ignore it. Let's look at the type of friendships you are in and how your friends treat you. This will tell you what you think of yourself.

If you are always with people who don't treat you with love and kindness — forget about what kind of people they are — look at who **you** are. Why would you be in a relationship with anyone who treats you poorly? Often it's because you don't think you deserve to be treated better. If you liked yourself, you wouldn't hang around mean people. If you thought you were okay, you wouldn't even think twice about discontinuing a friendship with someone who mistreated you.

When you have self-esteem and like yourself, you don't allow people to treat you badly. When I was in the ninth grade, I started hanging out with a girl named Stacey. She was a lot of fun to be with and we had a lot in common. The problem was that when we were together and her other friends would come around, she would totally ignore me and act like I wasn't there. When she did speak to me she would say rude things to me. So I put up with it for a while, until finally one day I just thought, I deserve a better friendship than this. I don't want friends who treat me this way. So the next time she called me to do something, I just explained to her that it made me feel bad when she would treat me the way she did around her other friends. I didn't want to be her friend anymore if that was the way she was going to treat me. Her reaction really surprised me. She said, "Wow, I'm sorry. I didn't realize I was treating you that way. I want to be your friend. I like you and I will not do that anymore."

Not allowing people to treat us poorly builds our self-esteem. When we say **no** to being treated badly, not only do we say to ourselves we are too good to endure a bad relationship, but also we allow good people into our lives to have great relationships with. Sometimes it's scary because we think that we might end up with no friends. Not so. It just allows room for better friends.

Walk through life doing what will make you proud of yourself. Self-esteem has to do with how we feel about ourselves. It's really simple. **Stop** trying to make others like you. Learn to make **you** like you. IT'S ONE OF THE KEYS! No matter how hard you try, not everyone is going to like you. For example, you go to school wearing those new dark green cargo pants that you really like and one of your best friends says she doesn't like them. So you stop wearing them and a month later another friend asks you why you haven't worn your green cargo pants. She really liked them! What are you going to do? Are you going to keep wearing the pants or not?

My youngest daughter bought a great yellow dress that came with thigh-high tights. It was different from anything she had ever worn. She got up the next morning to go to school, very excited about wearing her new dress. Since she usually didn't wear a dress, they all made a big deal about it. Some made fun of her and others were just shocked.

After school she told me how uncomfortable she was about all the comments and never wore the dress again. What a shame! Wouldn't it be a good feeling to get up in the morning and pick clothes to wear that you like, even if no one else does? What do you think your friends would think if they knew it didn't matter to you whether or not they liked what you were wearing? They might just respect your independence. I secretly liked the girls in school who dressed the way they wanted to and didn't care about what other people thought. They were unique. We are all unique. It's just that some of us are afraid to let our uniqueness shine. Be yourself, wear what you like, and make yourself happy! Allow yourself the freedom to truly be who you are.

Let's take a quiz to see how you are doing in the self-esteem area.

SELF-ESTEEM QUIZ

1. You are talking with some friends and one of them starts talking badly about a person you know who isn't very nice to people. You:

   a. Tell your friend about a time that person did something really horrible to someone.
   b. Get mad and walk away.
   c. Think really hard about something that person did that was nice and tell your friends.
   d. Just don't join in.

2. Your girlfriend has a boyfriend who is really cute and he is flirting with you and asks if you want to do something after school. You:

   a. Tell him you will meet him after school, but only as friends.
   b. Throw your milkshake in his face and start screaming at him about how horrible he is.
   c. Tell him you're not interested in him and that he is not being a good boyfriend to your girlfriend, and tell your girlfriend.
   d. Laugh because you are embarrassed. You don't really give him an answer.

3. *You didn't study for a math test, and you are sitting next to someone who always gets As. You can see her paper. If you want to stay on the honor roll, you need a B on the test. There's a question you don't know. You:*

   a. Just quickly glance at the girl's paper to get an idea of what the answer might be.

   b. Give it your best guess and hope it's right.

   c. Look at her paper and write the answer a little differently.

   d. Don't give it a shot. Leave it blank.

4. *You have a project in biology that you haven't started. It's due tomorrow, but your friends want you to go to the movies. You:*

   a. Blow off the project and go to the movies, telling yourself it won't affect your grade that badly.

   b. Stay home and give the project the attention it needs even if it means staying up late.

   c. Rush through the project so that you can go to the movie too.

   d. Stay home to do your project, but you are so upset that you're not at the movies you can't concentrate, but you try to do the best you can.

5. *You are at a friend's house after school, and she brings out a dozen chocolate-chip cookies to snack on. You:*

   a. Eat one or two cookies, and don't worry about it.

   b. Pig out on six cookies because you are starving.

   c. Eat as many cookies as you want because you are really skinny.

   d. Get upset with yourself because you know you can't have one, you ate too many sweets yesterday. Say, "No thanks."

6. You haven't exercised for two weeks. You:

a. Tell yourself you are a lazy person a hundred times to make sure you don't ever do that again.

b. Realize that sometimes your schedule and life make it hard for you to exercise and just start back up with the exercise program.

c. Work out three times a day for five days to make up for the time lost, and never let it happen again.

d. Know that because you are young, your body won't be affected that badly, and work out when you can.

7. You know a friend keeps saying mean things behind your back. You:

a. Give her the cold shoulder until she figures it out.

b. Confront her, telling her you will no longer be able to be her friend if she doesn't stop.

c. Tell her you need to stop being her friend because she is saying bad things about you.

d. Just realize that no one is perfect and love her for who she is.

8. Your friend tells you she doesn't like the pants you are wearing. You:

a. Agree with her because you want her to like you.

b. Tell her you like the pants . . . that's why you bought them, and that it's okay if she doesn't like them. She doesn't have to wear them.

c. Think maybe she is right and give the pants to Goodwill.

d. Get a little upset at her, but don't say anything, and keep wearing the pants.

SELF-ESTEEM QUIZ SCORING

	#1	#2	#3	#4	#5	#6	#7	#8
a.	=0	=0	=0	=0	=3	=0	=1	=1
b.	=1	=1	=3	=3	=0	=3	=3	=3
c.	=3	=3	=1	=1	=1	=1	=2	=0
d.	=2	=2	=2	=2	=2	=2	=0	=2

If you scored 0–4: You have some work to do. Pay special attention to all of the sections that will help you start to build your self-esteem.

If you scored 5–10: Your self-esteem is low and suffering, but not hopeless. Keep reading.

If you scored 11–20: You have a good start on your self-esteem. After reading this book, I bet it improves. Keep working on it. You're doing great.

If you scored 21–24: WOW! You have great self-esteem. Keep practicing to keep it intact.

Think it over... and Journal

Write down some of the things that you are doing right now that damage your self-esteem.

_____

_____

_____

_____

_____

_____

_____

_____

_____

Now take a look at the list and see the next time one of the situations happen, try to change your behavior to a more positive response.

ACT LIKE YOUR OWN BEST FRIEND

Your intuition is that little voice inside your head that always lets you know what to do. Women are very special; our intuition is precise. Try not to be influenced by what other people think or say. Learn to listen and to trust your intuition instead. If you're listening to yourself, you'll never steer yourself wrong. Next time a situation comes up, tune in and listen to that inner voice and see what the outcome is.

Remember that everything you do, every experience, is a chance to learn. If you start doing something that makes you feel uncomfortable, pay attention to that inner voice. If you continue on and the outcome isn't to your liking, do some thinking about how you might be able to do things differently the next time. HEY! PAY ATTENTION! No, not to me, **to you**.

Also, remember that you're human and, on occasion, you're going to do things that don't make you happy. When you do, don't beat yourself up about it. Acknowledge the behavior as something you want to change, then work on changing it. This may take some time. That's okay! Just knowing we are working on ourselves makes us immediately feel better about who we are.

When I was about fourteen years old, I was hanging out with this guy I really liked. He didn't really do or say anything in particular but when I was with him, I always felt like something was wrong. I could never really pinpoint what the problem was; I just knew something was off. So I kept hanging around him until one day he didn't come to school. I found out later that he was picked up by the police for having drugs on him.

The great thing about being you is that you have a wonderful spirit with all of the answers inside. All you have to do is listen carefully to yourself, follow your intuition, and be your own best friend. Learn to trust yourself.

A Teen's Journey

So many times I haven't listened to my intuition and things didn't turn out so good, so I started paying attention to what happens when I make decisions by listening to my gut. Things work out so much better.

Think it over... and Journal

Can you think of a time when you did something uncomfortable even though your inner voice told you not to? Write about the event and how you felt.

_____

_____

_____

_____

_____

_____

_____

_____

_____

_____

If you start paying attention to that voice, your intuition, you will get good at listening to it. It will change your life.

Women have an incredible spirit. Do things in your life to help your spirit SHINE! When your spirit is shining, people are attracted to that vibrancy. When you do things that make you proud, when you like yourself, your spirit shines. And then isn't it amazing? People want to be around you!

So let's recap some of the things we have talked about that make us feel badly about ourselves and how to change them.

Problems: When you don't like yourself, you:

1. Talk badly about other people.
2. Do whatever you want, no matter how it affects other people.
3. Don't have integrity.
4. Don't finish projects you start.
5. Don't take care of yourself physically.
6. "Bad-talk" yourself.
7. Let the negative voice make you feel badly about yourself.
8. Have friends in your life that treat you poorly.

Solutions: When you like yourself, you:

1. Stop talking badly about people and say something nice about them instead.
2. Turn the tables to see how you would feel. Have consideration for another's feelings.
3. Realize that lying, cheating, stealing, and not having integrity makes you not like yourself and creates low self-esteem. So don't do it.
4. Finish the projects you start and take pride in your work, always taking enough time to do a good job.
5. Eat things that are good for you and that help you maintain a healthy body. Exercise regularly to keep your body fit.
6. Don't say bad things to yourself if you make a mistake. Learn from your mistake and appreciate the lesson.
7. Stop the negative voice and replace it with something positive.
8. Pay attention to how people treat you and set boundaries. Don't let them treat you poorly. If they continue to do so, let the friendship go.
9. Realize that no matter how hard you try you cannot make everyone like you. So you let that idea go and only do things that make you like you.

I LIKE ME, I DON'T LIKE ME

Try spending time with yourself. Take a look at what you like and what you don't like about yourself. See what you can do about the things you don't like and how you can strengthen the things you like. When I first did this at sixteen, I got a piece of paper and wrote down all the things I liked about myself and all the things I didn't. Here is what my list looked like:

Things I Like about Myself

1. I have a good sense of humor
2. I care about people
3. I'm good at taking care of sick people
4. My flat belly
5. My voice
6. My small feet
7. Always willing to try new things
8. My compassion for animals
9. I'm athletic
10. Positive outlook
11. Hard worker

Things I Dislike about Myself

1. Not smart enough
2. Too short
3. Thin hair
4. Bad complexion
5. Lazy left eye
6. Never great at any of my talents
7. Gossip about my friends
8. Always feel scared about being alone
9. Very forgetful
10. My teeth stick out
11. I never finish anything
12. Allow my friends to treat me poorly
13. Too insecure

Think it over... and Journal

Now, you make a list of those things you like about yourself.

_____

_____

_____

_____

_____

_____

_____

_____

_____

_____

_____

_____

_____

_____

_____

_____

Think it over. . . and Journal

Now, make a list of those things you don't like about yourself.

_____

_____

_____

_____

_____

_____

_____

_____

_____

_____

_____

_____

_____

_____

_____

_____

Let's spend a little time thinking about your dislike list. The things on this list really should be easy to change or accept. Sometimes if you can just change your perception of things, you can start seeing things differently. Let me tell you what I mean.

I wrote in my dislike list that I'm not smart enough. I am smart enough, but I just have to work a little harder at things. I have a learning disability. It's called "Attention Deficit Disorder." I have a hard time concentrating and staying on track. Having the disability doesn't mean I can't learn. It just means I have to spend more time *to* learn. If I have an exam to take, I have to make sure that I really know the information. I have to study more than most people. That is okay, because I know this. I do what I have to do to get the grade I want. Before I changed how I approached things that challenged me, I never felt smart enough, essentially, because I never studied enough.

Here's another one of my dislikes. I thought I was too short at five foot three, but as I grew older, I realized being short is okay. In fact, tall guys like short girls as much as they like tall girls. One guy will like me because I'm short, the next guy won't like me because I'm short. This goes back to being me and not caring what others like or don't like about me. I can only be me and not get wrapped up in what others think. Anyway, if I fall down it's not as bad as when one of my tall friends falls down. I'm closer to the ground, it doesn't hurt as badly. I think I can find a good reason for being either tall *or* short.

As for my hair, it's thin. So what! I have girlfriends who complain about their hair being too thick. Go figure! I figured out what hairstyle worked with straight, thin hair and got it cut that way. I like my hair now. My complexion got better too as soon as I started eating better and taking better care of my skin. My eye condition got better with age, partly because I started getting more sleep.

When I started asking my friends to treat me better, the funny thing was that most of them did. I stopped being friends with the others, which was okay by me.

My talents didn't develop until I was willing to put enough time into them. When I invested time into any of my hobbies, I became good at them. I wasn't good at the guitar because I never practiced, and then I quit. Did I expect to be a natural? Just pick up the guitar and be good? Fat chance!

When I turned the tables on myself about talking badly about others, I realized I didn't want people talking badly about me. So I paid attention to what I was saying about others and tried not to say mean things about them anymore.

As soon as I started being myself, I began liking myself. My insecurities lessened, and my fears about being alone subsided too.

I took care of my forgetfulness by writing things down. Now I always make a list of things I need to do. If I didn't make a list, I would still forget things.

My teeth, well, they still stick out. I've just grown to like my smile and decided not to get braces at this stage of the game. It was my decision.

I either changed or changed my attitude about everything on my dislike list. I found that everything on that list was completely in my power to think about in a new way. I am who I am. I have the power to change the things I don't like about myself and accept the things I can't change.

By changing my actions, like asking my friends to treat me better, I took something off my dislike list, because my friends didn't treat me poorly anymore. I was able to change my mind about how I felt about my teeth sticking out. Another turnaround was simply finding a hairstyle for my type of hair.

Most of the time, we dislike things about ourselves because we think we should look the way someone else thinks we should or the way people look online, in magazines, and TV. But one thing that I have learned in the last twenty years is my looks are not going to appeal to everyone. Beauty is in the eye of the beholder. Look around you. Have you ever noticed that some of your friends have terrible taste in guys? Well, those guys might be terrible to you, but great to your friends. That's what makes the world go 'round. Everybody looks different and everyone has different tastes. There are always going to be people you think are prettier than you and some that are not as pretty as you.

When I was fifteen years old, I was standing out in front of my house talking to a guy I was crazy about. It was a hot summer day. I was in shorts and bare feet. All of a sudden I noticed he was staring at my feet. He said, "My god, you have the ugliest feet I have ever seen! You should never go barefoot." I tried to act like it didn't bother me, but the reality was his saying that made me feel horrible. My heart felt like someone was using it as a punching bag. I didn't go barefoot for a long time. I knew that my feet maybe were a little wide but they didn't seem ugly to me until this guy made that comment. From then on, I was self-conscious about my ugly feet. When my girlfriends were buying cute, strappy sandals, I was buying sneakers.

A few years later, I was with some of my friends at a public pool and the subject of feet came up. My naked, vulnerable, and ugly feet started to look for cover. I began to sweat and feel insecure, and then, out of the

blue, a guy friend of mine said, "Deb has really pretty feet." I could hardly believe it. My feet were so happy to hear that! ME TOO!

It just goes to show you can't base how you feel about yourself on what others like or dislike about you. Doing this will make you crazy. Remember the story about my daughter's dress? Wouldn't it be terrible to walk around always trying to get acceptance from others instead of yourself? Base how *you* feel on what *you* think. Learn to love yourself first — inside and out, the good with the bad. One person's "bad" can just as easily be another's idea of what's "good." It's not **their** opinion of you that's going to make your life. IT'S YOUR OWN! Remember, that's the key.

A Teen's Journey

I used to compare myself to everyone and it made me feel really bad about myself. It made me feel so jealous of all my friends. Once I started realizing that everyone has things about them that are good, I started looking at the good things about me, and this has helped me like myself more.

It's easy for me to say that what's important is what's on the inside, but the reality is, at this stage of your life, the outside is also important. Just try to remember that our inside is what makes us SHINE.

Have you ever noticed sometimes you meet someone who you think isn't that hot, but then when you get to know him you find out he's special? It's like he's become hotter right before your very eyes. It can also happen in reverse. You meet someone you think is cute, but when you get to know him and find out that he's not very nice, his looks start to dull.

I know it is hard to believe, but what is on the inside is what makes us pretty, not what is on the outside. The better we feel about ourselves, the prettier we become.

Don't compare yourself to other people, especially the girls in all the magazines. That is not reality. Computer technology is amazing; it can make legs look longer and smoother and faces look flawless. Why compare yourself to anyone? You are unique. You are beautiful in your own way. After all, you are the only you in the world! And that's pretty cool.

Well, enough about the outside; just try to love yourself the way you are — thin hair, short, protruding teeth, with absolutely beautiful feet.

ARE YOU A VICTIM?

Sometimes we feel like victims because we are not willing to accept responsibility for ourselves and our actions. It is impossible to have self-esteem if you are powerless. VICTIMS ARE POWERLESS! Let me explain. If you *never* admit that anything is your fault or believe you don't have control over some situation in your life, how are you ever going to make any changes in yourself? If you think it is always someone else's fault, then *other* people actually control what happens to you in your life. That sounds pretty scary to me. Make no mistake; you don't have the power to change what anyone else does. You only have the power to change what *you* do. Here is a story I want to share with you.

I was sitting outside one night with my fourteen-year-old daughter and her friend Karen. Karen was visibly upset, and when I asked her what was going on, this is the story she told:

"A few weeks ago," Karen said, "My friend invited me to a sleepover at her house. She said her parents were going out of town and that it would just be her and her older brother, Max, for the weekend. I was a little nervous, because his friends were going to be there, too, and they always throw big parties with alcohol even though they're underage. I went to her house anyway, and Max's friends showed up with lots of beer. They kept trying to force me to drink. I said I didn't want to, but they wouldn't stop. I was so scared, I started crying and ran upstairs. I'm so upset Max and his friends did that to me."

After Karen finished her story, I asked her if there was anything she could have done that would have prevented the situation. Karen's answer was that there wasn't anything she could have done. So Karen, in this situation, decided to remain a victim. "They did it to me." She was powerless because she believed there was nothing she could do. That's a pretty scary place to be in life. That same situation could keep happening. In Karen's mind, the only way to change the situation was to change the boys' behavior. How hard would that be? IMPOSSIBLE! You can't change other people. That's correct, but you can change yourself. As long as Karen believed there was nothing she could have done, this same kind of situation could keep happening to her. She really believed she had no choice.

I talked to Karen about that nervous feeling, her uneasiness before going to her friend's house. Karen's uneasiness was her intuition (her "inner voice") letting her know she might be entering into a situation that wasn't good for her. Sometimes that voice is so subtle, you have to listen carefully in order to hear it. When I asked her if she had listened to that voice and not gone to her friend's house, would that have prevented the whole situation? Her answer was, "Yes, yes it would have." But she went to her friend's house anyway.

First, I want to say that what Max's friends did was totally wrong. If someone says No, it means No! So in no way am I saying that she isn't a victim of their actions. The part I want you to look at is her part in it. If she can own her part in not listening to her intuition and not going to her friend's house when she knew there would be drinking involved, she can prevent situations like this from happening in the future. Having confidence and satisfaction in oneself equals SELF-ESTEEM.

The biggest discovery for Karen was that she didn't need to be a victim, and that she had the power to keep herself out of uncomfortable situations. Knowing that she didn't have to be a victim gave Karen back her inner strength. Remember, before we talked there was nothing she thought she could have done. She was a powerless victim. Afterward, Karen was shining

with power. She was excited with her newfound strength.

Listen to your inner voice. Be honest with yourself, and don't do things that make you feel uneasy. It's what I call the "Power Circle." The more you do the things *you* want to do — things you know are right for you — the more confidence you will have. The more confidence you have in yourself, the less you do those things that you don't want to do, that aren't good for you. Does that make any sense? It's very strange, but it is true.

The lesson Karen had the opportunity to learn was first, she didn't have to be a victim. Karen had the power to avoid getting into situations that

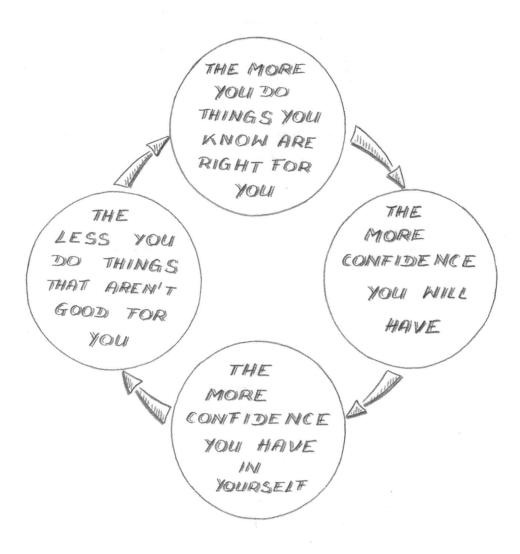

were not good or safe for her. Second, all of us must take responsibility for ourselves. This gives Karen the power to make her own decisions. Third, listen to your intuition, your inner voice. If Karen had listened to her inner voice, she wouldn't have gone to her friends in the first place.

Think it over... and Journal

Write down a time when you were in a situation where you thought you didn't have control, or where you might have been a victim. How did you feel?

_____

_____

_____

_____

_____

_____

_____

_____

_____

_____

_____

_____

It doesn't feel good to not be in control of your life, to be at the mercy of others, does it?

Think it over... and Journal

Now take that same situation and write down ways you could have changed the outcome by taking action, by not being a victim, and by listening to your inner voice.

_____

_____

_____

_____

_____

_____

_____

_____

_____

_____

_____

_____

_____

How does that feel? Much better, doesn't it?

If we play the victim, we will be totally powerless. Don't let things just happen to you. Instead, take control of the situation. Don't give away your power. It's amazing how many people I meet who blame people in their lives for everything that happens to them. They blame their friends, teachers, boyfriends, and parents. Look at every situation as if you have the power to do with it as you wish — because you do. You are not a puppet whom other people have control over.

Learn this as a teenager and you won't grow up to be a powerless victim. One of the best things I learned as an adult was that no one is to blame for things that are happening in my life. Not my boyfriend, friends, acquaintances, or my parents. I've made all the choices in my life.

A word or two about parents: they're people too. Parents do the best job they can. Like all of us, parents are human beings on a journey, learning about life. It was up to me to learn from my parents, no matter how they raised me. When I looked at Mom and Dad as people, I understood that they were learning lessons just as I was learning. I was not as hard on them after I realized that.

My oldest daughter told me that the day she realized I was a person on the same journey as her, maybe even learning some of the same lessons, she stopped viewing me as this perfect person who knew everything. She stopped getting angry every time I made a mistake. It's a hard job being a parent, trying to be perfect and knowing all the answers. Parents don't know all the answers. They are certainly not perfect. Love them for who they are and stop blaming them for your life. Stop being a victim.

The day I stopped blaming my parents for my protruding teeth, lack of talent, thin hair, and bad relationships with people was a great day for me. It was the day my life started to change and I stopped being a victim.

Powerless victims are easy to pick out: they seem weak, frail, and small. I once heard a woman comment that she had no musical talent because when she was younger her parents never gave her guitar lessons. Okay, but this was a thirty-year-old woman who hadn't lived in her parents' home for twelve years. She could have picked up a guitar and started taking lessons when she was on her own. Who was stopping her? Do you think that if she would have started taking guitar lessons twelve years ago, she could have become a good guitarist? I think so.

Take control of your life. Let's say you're at a party where you are beginning to feel uncomfortable. Kids are drinking, things in the house are being wrecked, and the party is getting out of control. You want to go home, but the girls you're with don't want to leave. The temptation might be to stay, but what if you said to your friends, "Hey, you can stay if you want to, but I'm going to go call someone to pick me up. I want to go home. This is a stupid party." The next day at school, one of your friends comes up to you and says, "When did you leave last night? You were lucky. The cops came by and broke up the party, and we all got in big trouble." So, they didn't think you are a geek for leaving, and even if they did, who cares? The more confident you are in the decisions you make for yourself, the more people respect you. And guess what? The more you respect yourself too. If people make fun of you, it has nothing to do with you. In truth, it's because they are feeling insecure about who THEY are.

If you don't feel comfortable somewhere, have someone come get you. Who cares what people think about you as you're leaving? If you act strongly on your conviction about not wanting to be there, your friends won't give you a hard time. You simply tell them, "The party is stupid. I just don't feel like being here anymore." If you have a strong sense of yourself, it won't matter what your friends think. In fact, maybe they are feeling the same way but are too afraid to say something. When you act like you're not afraid to leave, they may follow. You don't have to be miserable and uncomfortable in any situation. If you have a strong sense of yourself, you will do what is good and what feels right to you, no matter what other people think.

Another good lesson that I have learned is that I have the power to be anything I want to be if I work hard enough. I can master any skill if I put my mind to it, and I can prevent most negative things from happening in my life. I say "most things" because if a car hits me as it speeds down the road, and I didn't even see it coming, then that's pretty hard to prevent.

The solution to increasing self-esteem is to start liking yourself. Do things you like. Do things that make you proud. Stop blaming others for things that are going on in *your life*! Take a look at yourself, your actions, and how they apply to things happening in *your life*.

Having self-esteem is very powerful. When you have confidence and satisfaction in yourself, you make decisions that are good for you, like leaving parties that make you feel uncomfortable, or telling friends, "No thanks, I don't want to go to the party," or wearing the clothes that you like. Having self-esteem and liking yourself means others can't affect you. No one can say anything negative about you and hurt you because you are okay with yourself. You are dependent only on yourself for feeling good about your life. That is a comfortable feeling. If someone tells you that you have ugly feet, you can just smile to yourself and say, "I like my feet." You also aren't dependent on people saying *nice* things to you to feel good about yourself. When people compliment you, it's fine, but it's not like you need it to be okay with yourself. If you like and accept everything about yourself, you will just plain like yourself through and through.

THAT NEGATIVE INNER VOICE

Shhh! Listen! It can be totally quiet outside but it's so noisy inside of your head. Inside your head can be very loud with negative self-talk. The negative talk may not be so noticeable; you have to listen very carefully. Some people are aware of this voice and others have no idea it is there. So it's important to pay attention and listen carefully to what the voice inside your head is saying.

We all have this negative voice that makes us feel badly about ourselves. If your goal is to like yourself, this is going to be impossible to do if you listen to the negative inner voice.

When we start to pay attention to the voice and question it, it will begin to quiet down.

Here are a few negative things it can be saying.

- ❋ You're not good at anything.
- ❋ You're so ugly.
- ❋ You're no good.
- ❋ You're a loser.
- ❋ You're dumb.
- ❋ You can't do anything right.
- ❋ You're fat.
- ❋ You are going to fail.
- ❋ You mess everything up.
- ❋ You're not as good as they are.
- ❋ You're always doing something wrong.

If you had friends who were saying things like this to you, would you keep them as friends? No! But you hang out with this voice inside of you 24/7 and never tell it to stop. Not only do you not tell it to stop, you might even agree with it.

I think it's a good idea if you name this inner voice so you can separate it from yourself and let it know that it's not the truth about you and it's not okay to say those things to you. I picked the name Ralph because ralphing is a term for throwing up. Every time that negative voice says something mean to me, I feel like it is throwing up on me. You can use Ralph or pick a different name.

Ralph is like a bad friend who doesn't say nice things. I think having a name for this voice makes it easier when we hear it to be able to quiet it down by saying things like, "Hey, Ralph, that's a lie! I am good enough, I'm not a loser and I'm going to succeed, so back off." You have to stick up for yourself with Ralph just like you would if it was someone at school saying the same things to you.

The first thing you need to do is listen to what your Ralph is saying to you and write it down so you know what you are going to say to Ralph to make him stop.

What is Your Ralph Saying?

✸ _____

✸ _____

✸ _____

✸ _____

✸ _____

✸ _____

✸ _____

As long as Ralph is telling you these things, he will also be controlling how you feel. It is going to be impossible for you to feel good about yourself and have self-esteem if you continue listening to Ralph and believe what he says. The worst part is you will make decisions in your life based on what he is telling you. Here are a few examples:

Ralph: "You're not good enough." Action: You won't try out for soccer.

Ralph: "You're dumb." Action: You will get bad grades.

Ralph: "You're ugly." Action: You won't accept compliments.

Ralph: "You're always doing something wrong: Action: You won't try and you will likely be apologizing for things that aren't your fault.

See how this works? Ralph has a lot of control over your life. We all have a Ralph inside our heads. Now that we have identified him and how destructive he can be, what can we do about him?

Whenever you hear Ralph, that negative inner voice, you treat it like it is a separate person inside of you, not who you really are. You have to say to Ralph, "That's a lie and I don't believe you." Then you say the opposite of what Ralph has said. Here are some examples:

Ralph: "You're not good enough. You shouldn't even bother trying out for the soccer team."

You: "That's a lie. I am good enough and I'm trying out for the soccer team."

Ralph: "You're ugly."

You: "That's a total lie. I'm not ugly. I have some great features. Anyways, what makes me shine isn't my looks. It's what is on the inside and I'm a great person."

Are you getting it? You need to put Ralph in his place and tell him he is wrong every time. Don't let him tell you you're not good enough, you're ugly, or anything negative at all. Do it out loud when no one is around because it is more impactful this way. But, if you are around people, just say it in your head.

Once you stop allowing Ralph to run your life, he will quiet down because he knows you're not going to listen or believe what he says. This is also true for the people in your life. If you have people who tell you you're not good enough or say negative things to you, you just have to say in your head, "That's just not the truth and I'm not going to believe that." Or you can actually say that to them.

This takes a lot of practice! Talking to yourself will feel weird at first, but trust me, it works. You will notice your confidence starting to build and you will start to feel better inside. Think about how crummy you would feel if you had someone following you around all day saying mean things to you.

I want you to take the list of what Ralph says to you and put a positive spin on them, like this.

❋ You're good at math.
❋ You have a cute nose.
❋ You're good enough.
❋ You're a winner.
❋ You're smart.
❋ You can do it right.
❋ You are going to succeed.
❋ You can make things right.

✳ You're as good as they are at a lot of things.

✳ You learn from your mistakes.

Now take all the negative things Ralph says and make them a positive.

Positive Spin on What Ralph is Saying?

✳ _____

✳ _____

✳ _____

✳ _____

✳ _____

✳ _____

✳ _____

Start noticing how loud your Ralph is and start to tell him he is wrong. This is where you are going to find out how loud and persistent your Ralph is. My Ralph used to be really loud. Not anymore!

TWO

What Are You Afraid of?

 Are you afraid of anything? Most of us are. I found that if I listed those things that frightened me, they were easier to handle. The following is my list, not in any particular order, which I wrote many years ago:

Things I'm Afraid of

My mom and dad not being here

Not having any friends

Suffocating

Cancer

Being hurt by my boyfriends

Not having any money

Being alone when I get old

Not being pretty enough

Being out of shape

Not being loved enough

Having nightmares

Speaking in front of a crowd

Being seen without makeup

Doing something to embarrass myself

Some of my fears are just about the way life is. I knew that my parents at *some* point weren't going to be there for me anymore. When I was twenty-six years old, I went through a divorce. At the time I needed my mother most, she became very ill. Her death came just six months after my divorce, and for a time I thought that I might die too. I didn't. Actually I became stronger because I had to depend on myself more.

I also have continued to feel hurt in a lot of my relationships, and I'd like to talk to you about this. Why do we stay in a hurtful relationship? Maybe we are with a guy who doesn't treat us right, and we're trying to get him to change. Girls do this all the time. We think we can change boys, but we can't. The reason we try to change them is because we're afraid our relationship will end and that there will be no other boy who will like us. So if we can make them treat us better, we can stay in the relationship. The truth is that if we felt good about ourselves, we wouldn't be afraid to leave relationships that weren't good for us.

Remember when I talked about asking a friend not to treat me poorly, and if she stopped that would be great, but if she didn't I would have to leave the relationship? Let me tell you another story.

I had a friend named Beth, who was with this guy for a year in high school. He wasn't treating her very well. He would go days without returning her call, and when he made plans to be with her, he would cancel them to hang out with the guys instead. Beth was always complaining about him to her friends. She was always telling him to stop treating her that way, but he wouldn't listen. Finally one day, she told me that she was starting to feel better about who she was and that she deserved a better boyfriend. Beth had decided to break up with her boyfriend and stop trying to change him. She made the change instead. Good for her! Beth also said that after she broke up with him she felt even better about herself. There is that "Power Circle" moving again. If you keep doing things to make yourself feel better, your self-esteem gets stronger and stronger. It's not good for us to be in relationships with people who treat us poorly. One of the reasons girls put up with guys who are not nice is **because they have low self-esteeem**! If you liked yourself more, you wouldn't put up with guys treating you poorly. Why not just be with guys who treat you nicely?

The hurt can also stem from you and your boyfriend making a decision to stop seeing each other. Even though you know that it is in your best interest, you still miss him. Missing him is okay, but just don't confuse loneliness with wanting him back.

Another fear of mine is getting cancer. My mom got cancer and I used to worry about getting it too. Worry is weird. Think about it. I was worried about something that might happen to me in the future. It also might *not* happen. So let's say I spend a lot of time in my present life fearful and worrying about getting cancer. Sometimes the worry even makes me sick to my stomach, or prevents me from getting a good night's sleep. If I never get cancer, the worry was a waste of time. And guess what? If I get cancer, the worry was equally a waste of time. If I get cancer, worrying about it ten years prior certainly isn't going to prepare me for it.

Worry is just a plain waste of time. If something is going to happen, it's going to happen, and you'll deal with it the best way you know how. If you try to stay in the now, to be present today, even right in this minute, you'll be happier. Worry ruins the present moment. You can change neither the past nor the future. It is only in the present that you can affect your life. *Where are you?* Try to check in with yourself several times a day to see where you are. If you're suffering about the past you can't change or are worried about the future that has not arrived, **you're not here**. You have to make sure you're here in the present to truly enjoy life. If you are here, the relationships in your life will be better, and you will be happier too.

Another fear of mine was and still is speaking in front of a crowd. When it came time to speak I used to feel sick, and I would actually start shaking. One thing I finally realized was that if I prepared really well for what I was going to talk about, it helped. Also, the more often I made myself speak in front of a group, the better I got at it and the less afraid I was. If you want to grow, push yourself a little. Do the things that scare you a little. Take risks. Not stupid risks that could harm you; just do some small things that you're afraid to do.

I used to have a fear about going without makeup and having someone see me. So one morning I chose not to wear makeup to work, and I was also going to speak in front of about fifteen people. So it was a double whammy! The worst thing that happened was that some of the people asked me if I was sick. They said I looked pale. I just laughed. It wasn't so bad. It allowed me to be okay without makeup. I really felt so free.

Another one of my fears was embarrassing myself in front of people by doing or saying something that would make me look stupid. So one day I did cartwheels through a large shopping mall for about a half an hour — *in front of everyone!* People clapped and screamed, "Do it again!" I actually enjoyed watching their reaction. It was interesting. Yes, I felt stupid, but it wasn't that bad. Deal with your fears head on! What you will find out when you do this is that those things you fear most are not nearly as bad as your imagination makes them out to be.

By sitting myself down, looking at my fears, and figuring out how I would deal with them, I came to understand one of my strongest fears — not being loved enough. I realized that the more love I put out there in the world, the more love I receive. The love I'm talking about has to be unconditional. If I love without making any conditions, then love comes to me many times over. If the love I give is conditional, expecting something in return like, "I'll love you if you love me," it doesn't work. Just love, and love will find its way to you. Offering love when you don't expect love back actually feels very freeing and liberating.

Some of our fears prevent us from doing things that we might enjoy. Look at your fears and see if you can do something that will make them seem less scary. Walk right through your fears and face them. Keep getting up in front of people and talking, enjoy yourself without makeup, or do cartwheels through the shopping mall. Do whatever you have to, but stop believing in your fears. Fear often comes from the unknown. Once I realized that nothing serious would happen, the fear went away. Every time you push yourself through a fear, you become even more powerful. When we stop letting our fears run our life, we become very powerful women.

A Teen's Journey

I love volleyball, but for the last 2 years I wouldn't try out for the volleyball team because I was afraid the other kids would make fun of me because I wasn't as good as them. Finally, this year I thought "who cares what they think, I want to be on the volleyball team." So I tried out, and I was so happy because I made the team, and now I can practice volleyball all the time and get better. I don't know what I was really afraid of.

Realize that you have no control over some of your fears, like the fear of people in your family dying, although you do have control over how you will respond to the death. The death of a loved one can be very difficult. It leaves you feeling empty inside. When I started looking at life as a place to come to learn lessons from one another, even if it was through the death of another person, it became a little easier. When my mother died, I was twenty-six years old and I had just gotten a divorce, a time when I needed my mother the most. Her death was hard, although I learned in the process of dealing with life without her help how to take better care of myself. I always know she is somehow there with me through my journey through life.

Other fears you can tackle head on. Keep getting up in front of people and speaking until it isn't uncomfortable anymore. That's when you will start to see yourself grow. Keep pushing yourself to overcome your fears and you can keep adding to that "confidence stockpile."

Think it over... and Journal

Everyone has a secret list of fears. Make a list of all yours, then write down what action you can take to walk through them.

_____

_____

_____

_____

_____

_____

_____

_____

_____

_____

_____

_____

_____

_____

The fears don't seem as big when you really think about them.

Think it over... and Journal

Do something that is taking a risk, but not a dangerous risk, something that might push you or embarrass you, like cartwheels in a mall. Then write about how it made you feel.

_____

_____

_____

_____

_____

_____

_____

_____

_____

_____

_____

_____

_____

Doing things that we are afraid of is empowering, isn't it?

TEEN ANXIETY

Most teens experience some amount of anxiety because it is a fairly normal reaction to stress. For many teens, the pressure of final exams, important athletic competitions, public speaking, or going out on a date can cause feelings of nervousness and unease. Anxiety can increase your heart rate or make you sweat. This is how the brain responds to anxious feelings.

Anxiety is a difficult feeling to deal with. It may seem like you have no control over this feeling and it seems to come on when you least expect it. Although there are many reasons you might be having anxiety, some reasons might be:

❋ Having high expectations to succeed. Do you worry about your grades all the time? Do you put so much pressure on yourself to be the best?

❋ The world feels scary and threatening. With the increase in school shootings, drills and lockdowns in school, teens have a sense of fear about going to school. Just knowing this has increased a feeling of fear and anxiety in teens and parents.

❋ Social media. Are you constantly connected to your social media sites? It's not surprising that your self-esteem is so connected to what is going on through your Instagram, Snapchat and other social media accounts. Have you noticed when someone posts something about a fun party they went to that you feel a bit anxious? Try limiting your exposure to your social media accounts.

Do you experience:

❋ Recurring fears and worries about things in your day-to-day life
❋ Irritability over little things
❋ Your grades dropping
❋ Not wanting to be involved in school activities or social events
❋ Difficulty sleeping or concentrating
❋ Drugs or alcohol use
❋ Headaches, stomachaches, fatigue, and pain
❋ Crying often
❋ Upset with criticism
❋ Panic attacks
❋ Worry about things in the future
❋ Worry about making little mistakes
❋ Extreme test anxiety

Remember you are not alone with the way you feel; a lot of teens have feelings of anxiety and even have panic attacks. Don't beat yourself up for having them, it doesn't help.

If you experience any of these issues, talk to your parents or a school counselor about getting support.

Some things you can do in the actual moment of a panic attack or anxiety is to take three deep breaths. With each breath, relax your body and heart area. After your three breaths say to yourself, "I can handle this and if it's too much I will ask for help" or "I am safe and okay right in this moment."

Pretend you are talking to a little girl inside of you and calming her down. You might have to do this a few times, but it works. If the anxiety persists, again go talk to your parents.

I was having such bad anxiety around school and pressuring myself to get straight A's. I finally realized I can only do the best that I can do and that has to be good enough.

Think it over... and Journal

What makes you anxious and what can you do about it?

_____

_____

_____

_____

_____

_____

_____

_____

_____

_____

_____

_____

_____

Remember you're not alone.

CHAPTER
THREE

Big Bad Bullies

 My first exposure to bullying was when I was five years old, living in Connecticut. For some reason I was a target for bullying. I remember feeling threatened just walking outside my house. One bullying incident took place when these older kids in the neighborhood would pretend they were going to run me over in their car, while I was riding my bike. I remember feeling really scared and anxious all the time. Why did they think this was funny?

The bullying never seemed to stop until I was a sophomore in high school. When I was in 7th grade, a group of girls used to constantly shove me, tell me they were going to beat me up, and even went into my locker and took my things. It was so stressful for me I started having stomachaches and nightmares all the time and my schoolwork really suffered.

I never told my parents or a teacher, I just dealt with it, hoping it would stop. When I was a sophomore in high school I made some friends who stood up for me and the bullying came to an end.

Who are these bullies that are so mean and how come they enjoy bullying so much? Let's take a look at The Big Bad Bully, the bullied, and the kids who just stand by and either watch or encourage the bully. Are you being bullied or do you know kids who are being bullied? Are you a bully? Before you can answer these questions you need to know what the definition of bullying is.

Bullying is when someone picks on, hurts, or intimidates (scares) another person deliberately, over and over, who isn't defending herself or himself.

Here are ways of bullying:

* Attacking physically, shoving, tripping, or hitting
* Gossiping or spreading rumors
* Shunning (keeping a person out of a group)
* Getting someone else to bully someone for you
* Teasing in a harmful way, not just joking

Bullying can also be done through texting, and social media – Instagram, Snapchat, etc. This is called cyberbullying and includes:

* Sending messages that are threatening, harassing, humiliating, or embarrassing
* Posting nasty pictures or messages online
* Spreading vicious rumors or lies through email, text, or social media

So now that you know what bullying is, are you being bullied or do you know someone who is being bullied?

ARE YOU A BULLY?

Be honest; take this quiz to see if you have ever bullied anyone.

✻ Have you ever hit, shoved, or pushed anyone more than once, just because you wanted to?

✻ Have you spread rumors about someone through gossip, note exchange, social media, or texting?

✻ Have you made fun of someone in a cruel way by name-calling or making fun of his or her clothes or looks?

❋ Have you kept a girl out of your circle of friends, deliberately?

❋ Have you asked someone else to push, shove, hurt physically, or verbally abuse someone you don't like?

❋ Were you a part of a group doing any of these things, even though you didn't do it personally?

If you answered yes to any of these questions, guess what — you are or have been a bully.

Are you ready to admit you're a bully or have been? Everyone has hard situations and emotions to deal with. Maybe picking on someone helps you feel better for that moment because it takes your attention off of your problems. Maybe in your family it is normal to call each other names or fight physically. If this is so, it's still no excuse to be a bully. We have to be sensitive to others' feelings.

Maybe you have only bullied once or twice or maybe you don't think it's that big of a deal. If you are a bully and you don't think it's that big of a deal, I want you to really think about what it is like for the person who is being bullied. Even if you haven't been a bully this is important information for you: it will help you understand the effects so that maybe you can help someone who is being bullied.

HERE ARE SOME OF THE EFFECTS OF BULLYING

Kids who are bullied can experience stress, anxiety, fear, depression, loneliness, physical illness such as stomachaches and headaches, sleepless nights, and even thoughts of suicide. Can you imagine being afraid to walk the halls, use the bathroom in school, ride the bus, or walk home from school?

To live under this pressure can be too much for a lot of kids. Kids have actually taken their own lives because of being bullied, so if you think it isn't a big deal, think again. Think about what part you're playing in making the world a better place to be in. If you are bullying people instead of spreading good, you are spreading negativity by hurting others. I can't imagine that you are really okay with tormenting another person until they are so fed up that they might do something to hurt themselves, or even take their own life.

If you want to stop being a bully, try understanding how the person getting bullied feels. Step into his or her shoes and ask yourself, "If I was that person how would I feel?" Imagine waking up in the morning and knowing you will be pushed, hit, gossiped about, excluded by girls who used to be your friends, and receive horrible text messages on your phone. This is your life, how do you feel?

When I was bullied I felt like an outcast, someone who no one would ever care about or didn't even know existed. I feel very badly for kids who get bullied and I actually feel badly for the bully because obviously they have problems. Overall it's not a good situation, but it does inspire me to be nicer to others, for sure.

Think it over. . . and Journal

How would you feel if you were being bullied?

_____

_____

_____

_____

_____

_____

_____

_____

_____

_____

_____

_____

_____

_____

Not so good, huh? That's what I thought.

The people you are bullying don't respect you. They might be scared of you, but they don't look up to you. It may seem like they look up to you because they don't tell you how they feel, but that's because they are afraid you will bully them. Wouldn't it be better to have friends who truly liked you instead of those who are pretending to like you because they are afraid of you?

A Teen's Journey

I was bullied a lot in middle school and it took my confidence completely away. I think kids bully because they have low self-esteem and need to make others feel worse than them.

Wouldn't you rather be liked and respected by your peers? You could use your energy for good things like a leadership position in school.

I can't imagine that you are okay with people thinking you are a mean, uncaring person. If you want to change and you can't help yourself, go talk to someone like an adult who might be able to help you. Sometimes just realizing how bullying affects another person is enough to make it easier to stop. I am confident that you can make the necessary changes to help you become a better person.

You might want to apologize to a person you have been mean to or bullied. This would be a good way to make amends that would help you feel better about yourself. It's as simple as "I am really sorry for being mean to you, it's not how I want to be." Here are good websites that might help.

https://www.stopbullying.gov

https://kidshealth.org

Think it over... and Journal

Write down any time you think you might have been a bully and what you could do to stop being a bully. If you have never been a bully, good for you, just write down your thoughts about how a bully could stop bullying people.

_____

_____

_____

_____

_____

_____

_____

_____

_____

_____

_____

_____

It feels much better to treat people well instead of treating them poorly.

ARE YOU BEING BULLIED?

If you are being bullied or you know someone who is, just know you are not alone. A lot of kids are being bullied in school everyday. I know that this doesn't make your situation any better; I just want you to know you're not alone.

If you are being bullied, it is normal to feel afraid, scared, alone, angry, hopeless, and possibly have physical effects like stomachaches, not sleeping, and high anxiety. This is understandable. Being bullied feels terrible: I know and so do a lot of other kids out there. So let's talk about what you can do to stop or prevent bullying.

❋ **Tell your parents.** If they don't take the problem seriously, tell a counselor or teacher or other adult in the family. Explain to them how it is affecting you. I know this isn't easy but it's very important.

❋ **Watch how you hold your body.** Walk tall, holding your head up high with confidence. The way you hold your body will send a message that you are either vulnerable or not to be messed with. Bullies don't bother confident kids.

❋ **Don't react to their comments.** Bullies like to get a reaction from you, so just ignore them and walk away. If you act like you don't care, sooner or later the bully will probably get bored. If you can't walk away with confidence then use humor. Humor can throw the bully off guard.

❋ **Work on your self-esteem.** Bullies pick on kids with low self-esteem. Pretend to be confident until you are; having confidence makes you less vulnerable. Do things in your life to make yourself stronger emotionally and physically. Exercise is a good way to feel stronger. Take up martial arts or yoga.

❋ *Don't fight back.* This is what the bully wants and you never know how they will respond to it. You could get hurt and get in trouble if you use violence. Again, walk away or be assertive in your actions in other ways.

❋ *Stay close to friends.* Find out who your real friends are and keep them close. Bullies are less likely to pick on kids in groups.

Being bullied is one of the worst situations to deal with in school I can think of. School is supposed to be a safe place where you can learn. If you are in constant fear, it's impossible to learn.

A Teen's Journey

I have been bullied a lot in my life and it has really brought me down emotionally and physically. I wish I could explain to the bullies just how horrible it made me feel. It made me feel very worthless.

What do you do when you see someone getting bullied? Do you walk by like nothing is happening? Do you watch without knowing what to do? Do you run and get help? Do you participate in the bullying?

Believe it or not, your role is the most important one in bullying situations. What you decide to do when you see someone being bullied can change things completely. Most kids say they want to do something when they see someone getting bullied, but when it happens, they don't do anything because they don't know what to do. Even if the bully is your friend there are things you can do or say to stop the bully.

Most bullies like a crowd to watch them and the bystanders (kids watching) provide just that. You don't even have to egg them on, just doing and saying nothing while watching is egging the bully on. The bystanders usually feel very uncomfortable and want the bully to stop but are afraid to take action. If the bystanders disapprove, the bully often stops.

So as a bystander, if you think there is nothing you can do, you're wrong. What you decide to do can either encourage the bullying or help to stop it. Wow, your role is very important in the act of bullying. I believe that just watching the act is almost as bad as being a bully. Here are some things, as a bystander, you can do to help create a better outcome:

* ❀ Run and get a teacher or another adult, and inform them of what is going on. This isn't tattling, it's preventing something bad from happening.
* ❀ If the bully is your friend, make a comment like "Come on, let's not do this" and start to walk away. Sometimes this is enough to stop the bullying.
* ❀ Talk to your friends about what you would do if you ever see someone getting bullied, so that when it happens all of you can stand up together against the bully. The bully isn't going to bully a crowd.
* ❀ If you notice someone getting bullied over and over, bring them into your group, instead of leaving them out there all alone. Wouldn't you want someone to do this for you?

Kids being bullied have no chance unless other kids stand up for them. So, what are you going to do? What feels right to you?

A Teen's Journey

When I see someone being bullied I get this ache in my stomach. I just walk away cause I don't want to get into the problem myself.

This teen says he just walks away because he doesn't want to get into the problem. The problem is that he is already being affected by it; he has a stomachache, so his gut is telling him just walking away isn't right.

Think it over... and Journal

Write about how you would feel if you were being bullied and everyone was just watching.

_____

_____

_____

_____

_____

_____

Now write about how you would feel if you were being bullied and the crowd all came together and stood up for you.

_____

_____

_____

_____

_____

_____

Now you see why it's so important for you to take a stand, and stand up for the person being bullied.

Remember, if you think you are a bystander but you are either verbally egging the bully on or promoting the actions of the bully, then you are not a bystander, you're a bully too.

We need to start looking at our actions and realizing what a big part they can play in the world. The things we do and don't do make a difference. Sometimes we think because we don't do

anything that this gets us off the hook ("I didn't bully her"). Well, just because you didn't do the actual bullying doesn't mean you didn't do something wrong. Watching someone be mean and doing nothing is almost as bad.

A Teen's Journey

I feel so bad when kids get bullied. I think it is wrong, and I stand up for them no matter what, even if I don't know them.

If the people watching got together and either ran and got someone or stood up as a group and said, "Stop," the bullies would lose all of their power. That would be doing the right thing and is something to be proud of. Standing up for people who can't stand up for themselves is a great thing to do in the world and we should always be on the lookout for people who need our help.

OUR CRITICAL JUDGMENTS

Our judgments of ourselves and others are very tricky. Most of the time we don't even know when we are judging. We certainly feel it when we are being judged but we are a bit blinded by our judgments. Let's first look at what judgments mean.

Judgment: the process of forming an opinion or evaluation by discerning (noticing) and comparing.

Judgments aren't always a bad thing. We need to look at the decisions we make and judge or decide if it's right for us or not. The judgments I want to talk about are the ones we have about ourselves, others, and the world according to how we think things should or shouldn't be.

Judgments are everywhere and we have them all day long. We have judgments about our parents, best friends, teachers, people we don't even know and people we know really well like ourselves and most every situation going on in our daily life.

What would it look like if we were judging ourselves?

- ❋ I'm not as pretty as her
- ❋ My body should be different
- ❋ I'm not smart enough
- ❋ I wish I was taller
- ❋ My clothes are ugly
- ❋ My skin isn't clear
- ❋ I'm not good enough at soccer or other sports
- ❋ I'm not popular

These are a few ways we judge ourselves that can damage our self-esteem. If we want to be good to ourselves and love ourselves we have to stop judging how we look and who we are.

Let's look at some of the ways we judge others.

- ❋ She must be stupid, she's in a Special ED class
- ❋ I'm better than them because their skin is a different color
- ❋ She's weird because she likes girls
- ❋ She is heavy so I'm not going to be friends with her
- ❋ He's from another country; he isn't as good as I am
- ❋ I can't believe she wore that outfit
- ❋ Her clothes look so old and out of style

Think it over... and Journal

It's shocking to look at all the judgments we have about others. Think about all the judgments you have had about others today. Now write them down.

_____

_____

_____

_____

_____

If you judge others it's because you stand in harsh judgment about yourself. If you were happy with who you are, you wouldn't judge others as much. What are some of the ways you judge yourself?

_____

_____

_____

_____

_____

_____

Just looking at the judgments about yourself and others can help you not judge as much. One of the best ways you can shift your judgments is to first recognize when one comes up. Then say to yourself, this is a judgment I am having, and think about something positive about yourself or the other person instead.

Judging others and yourself is abusive and not kind. When you judge there is no place in your heart for love, not with others and surely not with yourself. When you are in judgment of yourself, your self-esteem takes a beating.

SELF ESTEEM

A Teen's Journey

It has been difficult for me because my parents are from Iran. People have said terrible things to me that have really affected me. I try not to take it personally but it makes me feel bad. I was born here and even if I weren't why would kids judge me for this?

How do you want to be in the world? Do you want to be a negative or positive force in the world? I would have to think you would want to be a positive influence and spread love. Just because people are different doesn't make us better than them. It just means we are different. When we judge others we are saying we are better than them.

So, pay attention to your judgments throughout your day, and start saying no to them and yes to love and self-esteem.

I invite you to take the day and actually count how many judgments you have about others, yourself, and any situation. Check in with yourself and see how it makes you feel.

CHAPTER

FOUR

Are You Creative?
Yes, Everyone Is!

 I believe creativity is very important and that everyone is
creative. When I hear people say, "Oh, I'm not creative,"
that just tells me that they have never explored this side
of their personality. Exploring various hobbies is one way
to stimulate our creativity.

When we first start a new hobby, we know very little about it.
Therefore it seems kind of difficult. A lot of times a difficult beginning
makes us quit. We assume we aren't good at it and never will be. In reality,
we *shouldn't* be good at it so soon. We're just beginning something new.
Now maybe you will be good at something at the very beginning like
sports, drawing, or music. If you're a natural, that's an added plus, but you
can't depend on having a natural ability in all the things in life. Most of us
need time and training to be good at something new. Occasionally we get
lucky and learn something quickly. But those times are rare.

Try everything that interests you, and give it a while to develop. Work
at it: take a class, whether it is photography, painting, drawing, sewing,
writing poetry, skiing, or even hiking. When I first started hiking, I hated

it because I was out of shape. I would huff and puff, and my face would get very red. A couple of times I said, "Hiking is not for me." I kept at it though, and now I enjoy hiking. There are trails that are still a little bit hard for me, but the more I hike, the easier it gets, and the more I like it. It's the same with all of my hobbies.

To find out what you like, try a lot of different things. Give them all a fair chance. After you have invested enough time and learning into each of them, pick the ones you like best, and then focus on them.

Think it over... and Journal

Write down all of the hobbies or activities that you have an interest in.

_____

_____

_____

_____

_____

_____

_____

_____

_____

_____

_____

_____

_____

Now, take your favorite hobby and give it a try. Join a class and stay with it at least through the class to see if it is something you enjoy.

Creating fills us with a sense of accomplishment and pride. A lot of times we're able to give our creations as gifts, and giving always makes us feel good. Have you ever felt bad about giving?

Creating relieves me of anxiety. It slows me down. I like myself best when I'm creating and giving. It's important to open yourself to creativity. If there is something you find yourself wishing you could do, *stop wishing!* Pick up a camera and go take a class or two, and you'll be able to take fun pictures. You will never know how good you are at something until you try. Just think how cool it would be for your friends and family to have photos that you had taken. Skill in a hobby can be developed if you put in the necessary time.

When I was younger I tried a lot of different hobbies. I tried baton twirling, flute, drums, guitar, painting, cheerleading, photography, gymnastics, sewing, baking, gardening, singing — should I go on? I didn't stay with many of them. At least I never stayed with some of them long enough to develop any skill. But all of the hobbies that I stayed with, I got pretty good at after some practice.

Whether you chose art, photography or crafts, writing poetry, gardening, or cooking, the act of creating allows you to have fun. It's a great way to spend time alone and have fun with yourself. Spending time alone getting to know yourself is important too, and being creative allows that. Sometimes it's fun to get together with friends, although I've found that I'm a better creator when I'm by myself. Alone, I depend on my own feedback, so my creations are purely mine. Of course, when you are first involved in learning a new skill, you most likely will be doing it with others. That's okay! However, planning some private time for yourself is critical to growing as a person. Creating gives you a tool to be alone, and find out who you are.

When we don't stay with hobbies long enough to get good at them, we think we are without talent, and that affects our self-esteem. When we are not good at things, very often it is because we never gave them our best shot. When a hobby became difficult for me, I would quit doing it. I never gave it my best shot. I was left feeling dissatisfied with myself, as though I wasn't good at anything. It's important to stay with hobbies long enough to give yourself a chance. When you begin to develop a hobby, stay with it even when it becomes hard, because it is going to be hard before it gets easy. When we stay with things long enough to get good at them, it makes us proud of ourselves. It helps our self-esteem. If we stop before we get good at something we think it's because we have no talent, which again, isn't fair to us. Not many people are good without practice. When we are good at something we feel good about ourselves.

SO GO CREATE, CREATE, CREATE.

Creativity is really important to me. Being creative turns a blank canvas into a work of art, a pile of boxes into a fort, and can eat away at your boredom or depression too.

Think it over... and Journal

From the list of hobbies on your last journal page, write down four of your favorites and list two places to go to help you get started.

_____

_____

_____

_____

_____

_____

_____

_____

_____

_____

_____

_____

_____

_____

NOW, GO GET STARTED!

CHAPTER
FIVE

Being Healthy—
Both Physically and Spiritually

 If you are not taking care of your physical health, it's hard to feel good about yourself. Self-esteem is strongly connected to how we care for ourselves. If we are eating poorly, smoking cigarettes, drinking alcohol, or not exercising, we feel physically crummy and spiritually crummy too.

Let's talk about taking care of your body, the only vehicle you have to use to get around. Now your body doesn't have to be physically beautiful to get you through this life, but it had better be healthy. Everything we do today will show up in our bodies later. What I mean by this is, if I keep eating things like macaroni and cheese and potato chips day after day, in ten years, if I get sick, it could very well be that my poor eating habits played a major role in making me sick.

A good example of this is my own parents. My mother smoked cigarettes, drank a lot of coffee, and her diet consisted of peanut butter and jelly on toast and jelly donuts. She never exercised, she never drank water, and she was sick most of her adult life. She passed away when she was fifty-five years old. That's really too young!

My father smoked cigarettes, drank a lot of alcohol, and didn't eat healthily either. My father had health problems during his life, and he passed away when he was sixty-five. That's young too! My parents didn't get to experience life for very long. They died when my daughters were young. They would have enjoyed their grandchildren, and my girls would have loved having healthy, happy grandparents who were around for a long time.

I believe that each of us is an important part of the universe, and therefore I want us all to remain healthy for our stay on Earth. It is hard to accomplish the things you want to accomplish when you are ill.

EATING RIGHT

Do yourself a favor and feed yourself the right fuel. Eat well. I'm not a nutritionist, but there are some basics you can follow. Drink at least eight, eight-ounce glasses of water a day. Eat lots of vegetables (mostly deep-colored ones). Go low on dairy products, and eliminate foods that aren't "real." Read the label on a product. If it contains ingredients like "monosodium glutamate" or has some other words you can't pronounce, it might not be all that healthy. Real food is something that was once living: green beans, lettuce, broccoli, asparagus, zucchini, poultry and fish, apples, bananas, other fruits and vegetables, rice, and beans. Here are a few websites to give you some ideas about nutrition: www.Youngwomenshealth.org and www.Girlshealth.gov.

Talk to your parents about a new meal plan and buying healthier products at the grocery store for you so you can start eating better.

Fad diets aren't healthy. Eating right is. It is important that you eat enough healthy food so that your body does not go into starvation mode. Starvation mode is where your body thinks it's not going to get fed, and it doesn't take long for it to think that. When you are in starvation mode your body starts storing fat. Just missing one meal makes it happen. You might even start to gain weight.

I started watching my weight and the things I ate because I thought I was overweight. My friends said I wasn't but I thought they were lying so I kept dieting. I got so skinny that I had to go to the hospital. I realize now that I stopped eating because I didn't feel good about myself. I take really good care of my body now and know how important eating healthy is.

When you severely reduce the number of calories you eat, your body goes into this mode. Because the body is designed to protect itself from famine, it stores fat. Not eating breakfast, or even postponing lunch until 2:00 p.m., will put your body into starvation mode. Instead of losing weight on a very severe diet, you will stay the same weight and, in some cases, will gain. I used to carry extra fat on my bottom and my legs. After I started eating three meals a day and small snacks in between, I lost the extra fat. But be careful about the types of food you eat or use as snacks.

If you need help understanding diet and nutrition better, talk to healthy people you respect. Talk to your sports coach or your parents or go online and look up healthy eating habits for teens. Most libraries have good books with the latest nutritional information, but I find the internet has great information.. Also, if you think you are on the path to an eating disorder, tell someone! Don't let it get out of control. One common eating disorder is not eating enough and losing a lot of weight. It's called anorexia nervosa. You may not show all of the symptoms, but could still be in danger. The symptoms can be:

- ✸ Having a strong fear of gaining weight even though you're maintaining a good weight for yourself or are even a little underweight.
- ✸ Knowing that you are too thin for your height and build, and refusing to work toward your normal range.
- ✸ Thinking you are fat when actually you're below your ideal body weight.
- ✸ Continuing to see yourself at a normal body weight even though you are losing weight dramatically.
- ✸ Being disgusted about the way your body looks.
- ✸ Missing your period for at least three months — now this is really when it is getting serious!

Another eating disorder is eating a lot, and then making yourself throw everything up: bulimia nervosa. With bulimia nervosa you eat large quantities of food, not caring how full you feel. You're totally out of control. After binging on food, purging usually follows. Purging is making yourself vomit.

Symptoms are:

❋ Taking laxatives, fasting, or exercising compulsively.

❋ Sneaking food only to binge later.

❋ Eating large amounts of food in a short period of time, while being very secretive about the containers the food comes in.

❋ Going immediately to the restroom after a meal to throw up.

❋ Obsessing about exercise.

If any of the symptoms from either of these disorders resemble any of your actions, or possibly one of your friends, seek help. Help your friend find help. Talk to your parents or counselor. Just seek help right away.

Here are a telephone number and website for eating disorders:

National Eating Disorder Association
1-800-931-2237
www.nationaleatingdisorder.org

EXERCISING

If you want to take good care of yourself physically, it is also important to exercise. Any sensible exercise program will work. Walk a few miles every day or bike ride, dance, or play sports, or hike with friends. Speed-walk through your neighborhood!

If you are still in school, get involved in sports. Just do something every day to keep moving. If your body is strong, it will be easier to do the things you want to do. The only thing a weak body wants to do is lie down and watch TV. How much fun is that?

When I am exercising regularly, I have more energy. I get a lot done, and I also sleep better. Try increasing your exercising and eating right

for two weeks and see how much better you feel. See how strong and powerful you become. When I know that I am capable of physically doing most things that I want to do, it means that I am powerful. When I am eating wrong and not doing anything physical, I start to feel weak and powerless. It is hard to be powerful when you feel like sleeping all the time. **So get off the couch!!**

SKIN CARE

One thing that I always found was so important was taking care of my skin. Make sure you wash, tone, and moisturize your face twice every day. During this time in your life — eleven to sixteen years old — pimples can be a real nuisance. A lot of your complexion problems can be hormonal. It's never too early to start taking care of your skin. Find a cleansing

program that is natural and has no perfumes. Make sure you incorporate washing, toning, and moisturizing your face into your daily routine, just like brushing your teeth. Eating the right foods will help control pimples and help your skin glow. Also remember to watch out for the sun. I know it's fun to be suntanned. Just don't overdo it. Sometimes we associate a suntan with being healthy and having vitality. Just a small amount of sunlight is needed for the body to give you all the vitamin D you need. Fifteen minutes a day will do it. Far less than it takes to get a suntan! Sun tanning regularly or burning your skin can cause skin cancer in the future.

Things to do to avoid sun damage to your skin are:

✳ Stay out of the sun during the peak hours of 10 a.m. to 4 p.m.
✳ Wear a hat and clothing to cover your skin while you're out in strong sun.
✳ Wear sunglasses that provide 100 percent UV ray protection.
✳ Wear sunscreen with Sun Protection Factor (SPF) 15 or more.

STRESS REDUCTION

Stress can do quite a bit of harm to your body and your emotional health. Work on keeping your stress levels low. One way of keeping your stress levels down is by taking care of business. Don't let things pile

up. For example, if you have a homework assignment that is due on Wednesday, don't wait until Tuesday night to do it. Stress builds each day the work is not done. The stress the night before the homework is due can become so horrendous that sometimes you won't be able to do the work properly. When the quality of your homework is poor, you can begin to get even more stressed over the grade you're going to get. It's a vicious cycle. What happens to our self-esteem when we do a poor job? Exactly! It harms our self-esteem.

Just be committed to doing tasks you have in your life and do them with pride. That means you have to work on them far enough in advance to have the time needed to do a good job and complete the tasks. Have you ever felt like you have a million things that you need to get done, and you're not doing any of them? Sometimes we have so many things on our plate that we feel paralyzed. We don't know where to begin.

Think it over... and Journal

If your life is bogged down with things you haven't done, make a list of what you need to do and start to knock items off the list one by one. List all the things you need to do on the inside of this plate and as you take care of them, be sure to cross them off.

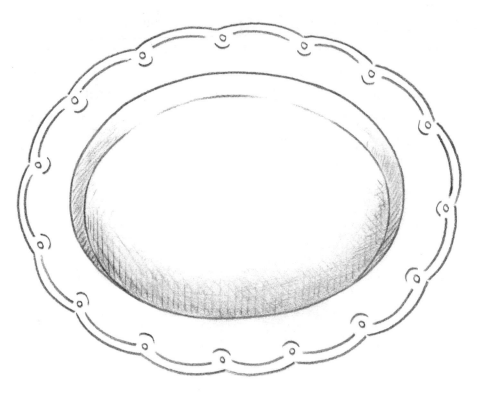

This may take a little time. Be patient with yourself, and concentrate on getting them done.

Never let that many things pile up again. Eliminate the jobs as they come, and don't wait until you have twenty jobs on your plate to start doing them. You'll be amazed how good it feels to start getting things off that plate. **No more stressing out. Take care of business!**

GETTING YOUR BEAUTY SLEEP

Another thing to help you achieve good physical health is getting enough sleep. Sleep is critical to a healthy life. Every night is a time for rejuvenation: Our bodies completely slow down and recuperate, so we can be strong for the next day. It's the time for our mind and body to let go of all that is going on. Can you imagine dealing with your life twenty-four hours a day? Think about never letting go of anything! When I don't get enough sleep, I have a hard time thinking. Life seems a lot harder than usual, and it's hard to concentrate. My skin also looks worse, I get bags under my eyes, and I don't have a healthy glow. Another thing I have noticed is that I stop sleeping when I have too many things on my plate and I'm not taking care of them. Also, if I eat a lot of sweets or a large meal before I go to bed, I have a hard time sleeping. It's important to pay attention to what you're doing so you can sleep at night.

So, let's recap the main keys to good physical health: eat right, drink plenty of water, exercise, take care of your skin, eliminate stress, and get enough sleep. All of these things keep our power shining.

SPIRITUAL HEALTH

Spiritual health is really important to our health and happiness — making sure we are always moving forward and growing. Growing means we're making the needed changes in our lives to become the person we want to be. That means being good to ourselves, to the people around us, and to the Earth. We need to be open to others' teachings, so that we can learn from them. We are all students of the world, but we are also teachers. This will help us to be good teachers for others too.

Teaching can be as simple as being honest with a friend and helping her to look realistically at her situation. Sometimes we refuse to see those things we don't like about ourselves. Friends then can be our teachers, helping to show us a mirror, so that we can look at ourselves more clearly. Real friends are not "yes-men." They don't always say "yes" to everything we do — especially when it is not the best for us.

When I was a sophomore in high school, my friend Tammy told me she kissed another friend's boyfriend. I told her I thought that it wasn't a very good idea; her actions were going to hurt our friend and ruin their friendship. I also told Tammy that it wasn't good for her either. Why would she want a guy who would cheat on his girlfriend? He obviously had no integrity. I asked Tammy what she saw in a boy who had no integrity and was a cheat. *It also made her a cheat.* If she was a cheat, how was she going to feel about herself and maintain her own self-esteem? She got upset with me at first and asked me why I couldn't support her and just be her friend. I said that if she wanted a friend who wasn't honest with her, who didn't want to help her grow, she might want to find a new friend. I wasn't her yes-man. She called me later and agreed she wasn't looking for a yes-man kind of a friend at all, and she thanked me for being honest with her. We became even closer after that. Be a real friend and let your friends know how you truthfully feel. It takes more energy, but in the end it will help your friend grow and help your friendship grow too.

You must also be real with yourself about the things you do that aren't in your own best interest. Allow people into your life who are up-front and truthful with you. There are a lot of people in the world who surround themselves with yes-men. Unfortunately, the ones who do are people who never grow. They remain unsure of themselves because they never face reality. Their yes-men friends never get in their faces and tell it like it is. I believe the reason that people don't tell the truth to friends is because they are afraid of losing the friendship.

I remember a girlfriend of mine in her twenties who was having sex with a lot of guys without protection. I was always talking to her about the dangers. First, I was really concerned about how many guys she was having sex with and, second, I was very worried that she was not using condoms. She was not willing to look at herself and grow and, therefore, she eventually stopped being friends with me. It was okay with me because I want people in my life who allow me to be truthful about how I feel. I always want my friends to hear the truth and be the kind of people I can count on to tell me the truth too. If friends don't have honesty and trust between them, then what do they have? NOTHING!

When people confront you in a loving way, no matter how difficult the situation is, they hold a mirror up in front of you. This kind of friend is a gift because she allows you to take an honest look at yourself and be real about the situation. You can choose to look at yourself and grow or you can choose to get upset with your friends and *not* look at yourself.

A Teen's Journey

The most important quality in a friend is loyalty, just being there for me no matter what. To support me with whatever changes I make in my life and to tell me when I am making the wrong ones.

The beauty about the mistakes we make is they can either be mistakes we keep making or they can become the lessons we learn from those mistakes. We will keep making the same mistakes until we learn from them. Mistakes are like a hot stove. How many times will you need to touch the burner before you realize it's *hot*?

Spiritual health is also obtained by taking care of business. Don't let issues with other people stew inside of you. It can make you sick, both now and in the future.

I once talked to a good friend Barbara about her alcohol problem. I explained to her how uncomfortable I felt to be around her when she was drinking and how I knew her excessive drinking was hurting her. Barbara's grades were dropping. She seemed to care less and less about herself. I told her that I was there for her if she wanted to quit, but if she kept drinking, regretfully, I was going to have to stop being friends with her. That was one of the hardest things I ever did in my life. In the long run my

honesty was good for me and good for Barbara too. At first we stopped hanging out because she was mad about what I had to say about her excessive drinking. She said she didn't have a drinking problem. Then after about a month she called crying and said she wanted to stop drinking. She wanted us to be friends again too.

So my actions to take care of myself actually helped my friend take care of herself. Being honest with friends is always the best route to go. What a gift I gave Barbara by being honest. I hope all my friends are that honest with me.

Think it over... and Journal

Has there been a situation in your life where you have tried to be honest with a friend about something she was doing that bothered you? Write down what happened when you talked to her and how it made you feel. Did it have a positive or a negative outcome?

_____

_____

_____

_____

_____

_____

_____

_____

_____

_____

_____

It helps to check in with ourselves, to make sure we are making good decisions.

If someone is affecting you in a negative way, talk with that person about what's bothering you. But do yourself a favor: Don't think that you'll get her to change. Chances are she won't. Talk to her because it will make *you* feel better and clear the air between the two of you. And it is okay to remove yourself from an unhealthy situation.

If you are uncomfortable at a party where people are doing drugs or you are feeling bad when you hear a group of friends slamming another friend, this means that your intuition is kicking in. **Listen to it, it's pretty smart!**

It is important for each of us to surround ourselves with people who are trying to improve themselves too. These are the people who not only allow *us* to improve *our*selves, but they also encourage us to grow and become the best we can be.

SISTERHOOD

Have you noticed the difference between the way girls treat each other and the way boys treat each other? Boys seem to have a certain unspoken brotherhood — a brotherhood that has rules like: They stand by their friend's side no matter what. A girl can't even come between them. They never get jealous about the way each of them looks. Boys never get upset if one of the boys gets more attention than another. They are usually just happy they are getting attention as a group. They don't argue about little things. They certainly don't shun each other. They are generally open to new boys coming into their group and hanging out. They think the more the merrier. They just get together and have fun.

Girls on the other hand — wow, we can be downright mean and nasty!

If one of the girls looks really nice and is getting attention, "the claws come out" and the other girls might start talking about her behind her back. Girls' insecurities can show up in mean ways. Girls rarely let a prettier girl into their group. In fact, they might not let *any* other girl into their group. They may become afraid that if they let the new girl in, one of them might get inched out of the group. When girls argue about things — which they do — they argue over the smallest things, and they don't get over it easily. They will end a friendship over a tiny argument. Some will also give up another girlfriend for a guy in a heartbeat. A guy would never give up a friend for a girl.

So, why do we do these things? Is it because we don't feel good about ourselves? It always comes back to this, doesn't it? If we felt good about ourselves, we wouldn't be insecure about other girls. When we get older, we realize our girlfriends are so very important to us. They understand us better than any guys do. We start to see that guys come and go in our lives, but our girlfriends are with us for a long time.

A Teen's Journey

I lost a good friend because I started liking her ex-boyfriend right after they broke up. I thought having him as a boyfriend was more important than her friendship. Boy was I wrong. We broke up two weeks later, and my friend doesn't trust me anymore and doesn't want to be friends. That was a hard lesson.

Sisterhood is a powerful bond between girls. Pay attention to how you and your friends treat other girls. Make some changes if you need to. Always turn the tables and see how it would feel to be treated poorly by one of your sisters. We all can remember a time when another girl was acting like we were a disease and telling people not to go near us. It felt like the world was coming to an end. Try to remember that feeling. Then before you treat another girl poorly, tap into that feeling. *You* be the one who stops this negative pattern. Help your friends to realize how mean it is and how it affects other people. Girlfriends are special, and the relationships you create with them make your life so much better. Also, having a lot of girlfriends is much more fun than just having one. If you have a lot of girlfriends, you always have someone to hang out with, and hanging out with a lot of girls is fun.

So, just start watching how you treat girls and help your friends do the same. The more you work on your own insecurities the more you will be able to accept other girls as friends, and not as a threat to you.

Think it over... and Journal

Name a time when a girlfriend treated you like a disease and write how it felt.

_____

_____

_____

_____

_____

_____

_____

_____

_____

_____

_____

_____

_____

Remember, that's how other girls feel when you do it.

CHAPTER
SIX

Be Cyber-Smart

 Wow! This is a whole new world and a whole new way of expressing yourself through texting and social media (Instagram, Snapchat, and TikTok, to name a few). Although these resources have great benefits like being able to communicate with more people, faster and easier, they can come with big problems. We want to be aware of the dangers so we can avoid them while still being online and using our phones.

Not being face-to-face may have some downsides we don't think of, such as not being able to see someone's facial expressions and not being able to hear their tone of voice. A friend might text you something that you take the wrong way and then you respond and she gets upset. Before you know it, you're in an argument about something that's not even happening. Has this happened to you?

We are going to look at different ways you can communicate and develop relationships, and the pros and cons of each. If you are aware of all the issues involved, then you can navigate with safety and security.

A Teen's Journey

My best friend and I didn't speak for a week because I had sent her a text about this guy she liked and I said he would *probably* like her back. Well, she took the *probably* like I said probably not. She thought I was saying that he was too good for her, and that's not what I meant at all. It took a week to mend things from that.

SOCIAL MEDIA

I love my social media sites, but I mainly use mine to let people know about *My Feet Aren't Ugly* and how I mentor teens and parents. Personally, I don't like communicating with my friends through social media because I'd rather see them face-to-face, but I realize that there are many people who enjoy communicating with their friends this way.

Think it over... and Journal

Write down the ways you communicate: texting, phones, Instagram, Snapchat, etc. What are the good things about them and the bad things?

_____

_____

_____

_____

_____

_____

_____

_____

_____

_____

_____

_____

_____

Take a look at how you might minimize the bad things that can come with the way you communicate.

A Teen's Journey

Technology isn't good for me because I forget about other things that are important. I get addicted to it and stay in the house all the time instead of doing things outside with my friends.

Let's make sure we are being smart about social media. Here are some tips for Instagram, Snapchat, TikTok and other social media platforms.

- ❋ ***Making your own page.*** This is a great way to express yourself and be creative. It's fun to design a page that reflects who you are. But make sure you are being true to yourself and your page is honest.

- ❋ ***Use an appropriate profile picture.*** Don't try to look sexy. You don't want to appeal to the wrong people or give the wrong impression.

- ❋ ***Limit your "friends" to the people you know*** or someone your friend knows really well. You don't want strangers reading about what you and your friends are up to. If a stranger does contact you, remember that you don't know who this person is. Don't communicate with them. If they continue to contact you, tell your parents.

- ❋ ***Never ever meet anyone in person.*** The only way someone can physically harm you is if you are in the same place together.
- ❋ ***Don't post personal information*** like your phone number, address, or what you will be doing during the day or that night. Make sure you ask your parents to help you with the appropriate privacy settings and security passwords so strangers can't see your information.
- ❋ ***Be kind online.*** Treat people the way you want to be treated. If people are being mean ignore them or use privacy tools to block them.
- ❋ ***Be careful what you post.*** Everything you post is there forever and you can never take it back, so think before you post photos, private details, or a mean comment.
- ❋ ***Click other links with caution.*** Social media accounts are regularly hacked. Look out for language or content that does not sound like something your friend would say.

Using social media can be a lot of fun. You just need to be aware of the dangers and take them seriously.

A lot of the same issues apply to the use of your phone and texting. Remember that what you send through your posts or texts can never be undone. If you send a friend a sexy picture of yourself you think is funny, know that she might not always be your friend and months down the road she might send your picture to people who you don't want to see it.

Ask yourself "Do I want the entire school to see this picture?" If the answer is NO, then don't send it.

Sending nude or sexy pictures over your phone is called sexting. There have been situations that have ended tragically due to sexting. One girl sent a topless photo of herself to her boyfriend, and his friend found it on his phone and sent it out to a lot of people in school. The kids at school started calling her names and bullying her until she couldn't take it anymore and took her own life.

This is such a terrible situation and it upsets me even to write about it, but I want you to know how serious this really is. You just never know where your texts are going to end up.

Think it over. . . and Journal

Have you ever sent or posted something that you wish you hadn't? If so, write about how it affected you or the other person.

_____

_____

_____

_____

_____

_____

_____

_____

_____

_____

_____

_____

Even when things seem funny to us, they can still be hurtful.

When you're sending a text to someone think about if it's okay for anyone else to see or read it. If it's not, simply don't send it.

One of the girls in my Girl's Circle lost a friend because she texted another friend what she thought was just a joke about her friend and the other girl forwarded it. Even though she was joking, it hurt her friend's feelings and she stopped being her friend. There was nothing she could do to convince her friend it was just a joke. What is a joke to you might not be so funny to someone else.

Here are some guidelines about staying safe on social media:

- ❋ *Never give out personal information* and use a nickname, not your real name.
- ❋ *Think before you send your message.* Remember that once you send it, you can't get it back.
- ❋ *A stranger is a stranger,* even if they're online. Don't trust anyone you talk to and again, never share your phone number, address, passwords, email address, where you go to school, or anything personal about yourself.
- ❋ *Never, ever, meet a stranger in person* even if they seem nice and you think you've gotten to know them. You don't know them! And you don't know if they are being truthful with you.
- ❋ *Get off the site* if you feel uncomfortable at all. Save the conversation before you leave. Tell your parents right away. Block the user and never communicate with him or her again.

Never communicate with strangers over social media and the internet.
Take this seriously — you never know who you are chatting with.

CYBERBULLYING

Cyberbullying occurs when someone under the age of 18 harasses, threatens, humiliates, or embarrasses, more than one time, another minor through the internet, phone, social media, or other digital devices.

Have you ever been bullied online? Are you a bully online? It's not okay to bully someone just because you don't know that person or you aren't standing face-to-face with him or her. Cyberbullying is as damaging as face-to-face bullying.

If you are being bullied online or want to prevent online bullying, here are some helpful tips:

❀ Ignore what is being said. Don't react. Remember, that's what bullies like. Your reaction makes them feel powerful. Don't respond, which means don't text, email, chat, or respond to a comment through social media.

❀ Don't gossip or write mean things about others. It can make you a target for being bullied.

❀ Be nice online and create an environment that feels good to be in.

❀ Tell your parents if you are harassed online. If you can't tell your parents, tell another adult that you trust, such as a school counselor. Ask that person to report the bullying anonymously, which will mean that the bully won't know it's you.

❀ Save all the comments the bully sent to you so you have evidence of the bullying. Even though it might seem minor now, it could get worse.

❀ If you are watching the bullying, even online, you are a bystander. Realize that you are playing an important part and that by doing nothing you empower the bully. If you can't stop the bullying at least you can offer support to the person being bullied.

Here's a quiz to see what you know about cyberbullying. Circle the T if it's true and F if it's false.

What do you know about cyberbullying?

T or F It's cyberbullying if a girl from school texts you saying a friend of yours is ugly.

T or F It's cyberbullying if someone texts you and says "I hate you" more than once.

T or F It's cyberbullying if you're playing an online game and one of the players says, "I'm going to get you."

T or F You should tell your parents if you get a message from someone you don't know asking for your address.

T or F You get a message from a girl at school saying mean things, so you should save the message.

If you circled true on all of these, good job! You have a great idea of what cyberbullying is. If you have friends that might not know, share this chapter with them and help them learn about it. Here is a good website on the subject: www.stopcyberbullying.org.

One of the girls I mentor, Kati, received a message from a friend on her Facebook site that called her names, criticized her body and looks and said some pretty horrible things for everyone to see. This message came from a casual friend of hers. The school got involved, the girl apologized and actually tried to become friends again with Kati. Kati is not responding to any emails or texts and she has removed the girl from her friends list on Facebook. She has no desire to ever be friends with this girl again.

Remember, you can't take anything back — not words, not photos, and not comments you think of as jokes.

A Teen's Journey

I lost a friend and actually a few friends because in a moment of anger I sent a message for everyone to see on Facebook and said some pretty mean things about her.

CHAPTER
SEVEN

Who Is Doing Drugs?

 What I have noticed in my years of talking with kids is that the kids doing drugs and alcohol are lost. They are the ones looking for anything to fulfill them. They are not quite sure of who they are yet. For these kids, drugs and alcohol are ways of escaping their lives instead of dealing with them. I group alcohol with drugs because I believe it is as dangerous as drugs when done in excess. If we work on liking ourselves and getting to know who we are, there will be no need to escape. In other words, if we create a life we enjoy living, we will have no reason to wish to escape from it.

Curiosity might be a reason for experimenting with drugs. Have you ever heard the saying "curiosity killed the cat?" This couldn't be more true when it comes to drugs, because there are drugs out there that can kill you with one-time use. Curiosity is great except when the action might be dangerous. Peer pressure might be another reason we start doing drugs. If we are caving into peer pressure we have not yet developed a strong sense of who we are. Again, if we don't have the strength to tell our friends, "No thanks, I'm not into drugs," when we really don't want to do them, what exactly are we lacking? Yes, self-esteem.

A Teen's Journey

One time some kids at our teen center asked me if I wanted to get high with them and I said I had to go to the bathroom and just left. It was easier than explaining that I don't do drugs. I would like to just tell them no thanks, I don't get high, but I'm afraid of what they will think of me.

It's great that she didn't give in and do the drugs; at least she got herself out of the situation. Wouldn't she have felt better about herself if she was confident enough to say what she wanted without caring what others think?

A friend of mine told me a story about her daughter, Jamie. Jamie was at a friend's house one night, and some guy came up to her with crack and was trying very hard to get her to do it with him. Jamie kept saying nicely that she really wasn't into it but thanks anyway. Well, he just wouldn't let up, and finally Jamie went off on him. When they were alone she started getting on his case. "What's the deal? Why is it so important that I get high with you? Why will it make you feel better if we do it together?" She went on. "If it's so great why are you giving it away, and why would I want to burn my brain with you? It doesn't sound that great to me, so cool it and leave me alone." She said he just sat there and stared at her for a long time, and then he finally left. She found out later that he was telling someone that he was done "burning his brain" with crack. Drugs are only cool to the people hooked on them. Believe me, they would rather be happy about their lives and not dependent on drugs to make them happy.

There are so many different kinds of drugs available today: marijuana, MDMA (known as ecstasy), cocaine, methamphetamine, steroids, heroin, nitrites, poppers, LSD, mushrooms, inhalants, and over-the-counter drugs. None of these do any good for your body or soul. Each one does damage in its own particular way. Over-the-counter drugs and household products are having horrible effects on teens when used.

One big problem with drugs is that a lot of them are made in a home lab with someone mixing the ingredients (a guy probably high out of his gourd). No, thank you! Drugs can kill people; one that doesn't affect one person might hurt someone else. We are all different. Not all drugs will kill you, but some will, and the others can mess up your nervous system and just take away your desire to live.

We're not going to talk about the benefits of these drugs because there aren't any; feeling different for a few minutes to a few hours isn't worth the risk. What we are going to talk about is what these drugs are, their risks, and the damage these drugs can do. It seems like a lot of people are doing drugs and you can find them pretty easily. You might be tempted to try drugs for the pure excitement, peer pressure, or need to escape troubled times, but before you go casually trying any drug you better be informed of the risks involved and know that you could be risking your **life**.

A Teen's Journey

I don't do drugs but I have anxiety about telling people no when they ask me if I want to do them. This guy in line at lunch asked me if I wanted to go get high, and I was so proud of myself for saying no with confidence, even though it made me nervous.

Before we get started on the specific effects drugs can have, you should know that this is really important information and it can feel pretty dark and heavy. This is a serious subject and there is no making light of it. I'm sorry if it feels disturbing — drugs *are* disturbing.

The substances in drugs change the way your body works. When you take drugs by smoking, inhaling, injecting, or swallowing them, they go into your bloodstream and travel to your brain. Their effects will depend on the amount or strength taken and how your body handles them, having to do with your size and weight, if you have eaten or not, and how your body processes the drug. You will never know how a drug is going to affect you from one time to the next. One person may do a certain drug and not have many physical affects; another may do the same drug and have a seizure and die.

Under the influence of drugs, you may do things you wouldn't normally do. I heard of a teen doing crack cocaine and not knowing where he was, and he jumped out of a five-story building, thinking he could fly. Call me crazy but that doesn't sound like much fun to me.

A Teen's Journey

I never realized how many people get affected by someone doing drugs until my brother got into them and it took my family down. My mother was depressed for a long time. You think it only affects you, but you're wrong.

This is so true. When you do drugs the effects don't only affect you; they will affect your family and friends too.

Here are the descriptions and the negative effects (risks) of different popular drugs. Some of them can be life threatening. I'm not going to go through all of them because there are way too many.

If you want more information here are a few websites:

https://kidshealth.org

http://www.teenoverthecounterdrugabuse.com

Crack Cocaine: Cocaine in a form that is smoked, not snorted, like regular cocaine. It is highly addictive and addictions seem to develop more quickly when smoked than when snorted. The risks of cocaine and crack cocaine include constricted blood vessels, increased temperature, heart rate, and blood pressure, risk of cardiac arrest (your heart stops beating), and seizures. With crack cocaine additional risks are acute respiratory problems — coughing, shortness of breath, lung trauma, and bleeding. Crack cocaine can also cause aggressive and paranoid behavior.

Crystal Meth/Methamphetamine/Crank: A highly addictive drug. I have heard of situations where someone has become addicted from first-time use. This drug can cause diarrhea, nausea, excessive sweating, loss of appetite, insomnia, tremors, jaw clenching, agitation, irritability, panic, violence, and confusion. It also causes an increase in blood pressure, body temperature, heart rate, blood sugar levels, and constriction of artery walls.

If crystal meth is used too much it can cause brain damage, a sensation of crawling flesh, paranoia, hallucinations (seeing things that aren't there), delusions, tension headaches, muscle breakdown (which can cause kidney damage or failure), and death due to a stroke or cardiac arrest.

This is a long list of risks because this is a very dangerous drug and the risks should be taken seriously. You would have to be crazy to experiment with this drug, knowing what the dangers are.

MDMA Ecstasy: Under the influence of ecstasy a person can experience deep heart palpitations and feel as though their heart is racing, and they cannot gain control of the sensation or their heart is beating out of rhythm, which could be a problem and could lead to a heart attack.

Another life-threatening issue is the change in body temperature people feel while under the influence. The body only works within a narrow range of temperatures. If the body grows too warm, the blood can clot within the blood vessels, and that could lead to a heart attack or stroke. If your blood is too warm, it can damage vital organs, including the kidneys. Some people end up dying while high due to the heat their bodies put off.

This drug more than most is made by drug dealers that don't care about the quality of the product, they only care about the money they make from selling it. Therefore you have no idea what you are really getting. Studies show that less than 35% of ecstasy sold is actually Ecstasy. Do you want to take a drug that you have no idea what it is? This is way to dangerous!

Inhalants: Items commonly found in millions of homes that aren't used for their intended use or according to directions can be deadlier than street drugs. These drugs are common household products found in garages and cleaning cabinets. The scary thing is that teens don't realize how dangerous inhaling these products can be. Some of the nicknames for inhalants are: whippits, poppers, snappers, and huffing to name a few.

Here is a list of products that could be deadly if inhaled: paint, spray paint, thinners and removers, gasoline, glues, felt-tipped marker fluids, household or commercial products like butane lighters, propane tanks, whipped cream dispensers, deodorant, hairsprays, vegetable oil cooking sprays, and static cling sprays.

Because the high a person gets from inhalants only lasts for a few minutes, some people may inhale over and over to maintain the high feeling. This increases the damage done to the body.

Inhalants cause many changes in the body by being absorbed by parts of the brain and nervous system. The short-term effects of inhaling these products are:

* nausea and vomiting
* slurred speech
* increased heart rate
* hallucinations (seeing things that aren't there) or delusions
* loss of coordination

With regular use of inhalants there can be long-term health effects:

* brain damage
* memory loss
* unable to learn new things
* muscle weakness
* depression
* headaches
* nosebleeds
* loss of sense of smell or hearing

The scariest thing about these drugs is that they can cause death from only one-time use. Your heart can beat quickly and irregularly and then suddenly stop, or instead of breathing in air you breathe in toxic fumes and stop breathing, or you could throw up and then choke on your vomit. People who are high often make bad decisions: they might try to drive under the influence, or do something irrational like jump off a roof. They could also get burned or start explosions if a spark ignites the flammable inhalant.

Over-the-Counter Drugs: Can be the prescription drugs in your parents' medicine cabinet such as cough medicine, pain relievers, etc. Just because these drugs are accessible and not illegal doesn't mean they're not dangerous. A prescribed medication for an adult could be life-threatening for someone half the size or someone with different medical conditions.

There is so much information available regarding over-the-counter drugs and I really believe in getting educated on this subject so you can make good decisions for yourself. When you make good decisions your self-esteem grows stronger.

These are just a few of the drugs that I believe teens are experimenting with more than ever. When I was younger I felt invincible, like nothing could ever happen to me no matter what I did. Sometimes we don't think about the risks of our behavior when we are teens, but this is a part of being young and not being mature yet. As we get older, we start to look at how our actions can affect our lives both in the moment and in the future.

A good thing to learn early is that everything we do in our lives creates an outcome that is either negative or positive. It's a good idea before we do things to look at all of the pros and cons of doing it. Ask yourself, "If I do this drug and there are big risks involved, is it a good idea?" If we look at the real risks involved, there is a good chance we won't do it. It's just not smart to go about our lives like nothing has a consequence when everything has an outcome — good or bad!

A Teen's Journey

I have seen what drugs do to people, it is very sad to me. One close friend is rotting away and giving up his passions and is changing for the worse. I am trying to be there for him, but I feel like it is a losing battle; he is really hooked.

Drugs are all around us and we have to make important decisions every day in order to care for ourselves. Drugs take us away from our own reality, which is the life we are living today. It is important to find happiness the natural way by liking who you are and doing things that are good for you. If you're unhappy, take a look at why and see if you can create happiness through a source other than drugs.

I think we all play such an important part in the world, and we need to be 100 percent present to create it the way we want. I personally don't want to miss something good. If I'm so high that I barely know my name, I'm probably going to miss a lot. Start saying "no" to things that aren't good for you like mean people in your life, boyfriends who don't respect you, sex for all the wrong reasons, and drugs.

Think it over... and Journal

Write down your feelings about drugs and what you see them doing to people. What is your view on drugs? If you are doing them, write down why you are, or if you have friends using drugs, why do you think they are doing them?

_____

_____

_____

_____

_____

_____

_____

_____

_____

_____

If you're doing drugs, don't be afraid to get help to stop. If you're not doing drugs, but know someone who is, help him or her stop.

ALCOHOL IS A DRUG TOO!

I have seen alcohol do as much damage as drugs do; just because alcohol is legal for people over the age of 21 doesn't mean there are no risks. Plenty of people ruin their lives through alcohol.

If you drink too much, you could get alcohol poisoning, which results from drinking large amounts of alcohol in a short amount of time. What is a large amount, you can't really say because it can be a different amount for everyone. When the body is poisoned by too much alcohol you will experience violent vomiting, extreme sleepiness, unconsciousness, dangerously low blood sugar, seizures, difficulty breathing, and possible death.

A Teen's Journey

A friend of mine was dared to drink a whole bottle of vodka and did it and got alcohol poisoning. He got rushed to the hospital and died a few hours later. It made me realize that drinking is so lame and that my life is worth more than that. I really miss him a lot.

Another risk with drinking is that you might think it's okay to drive, which could result in an accident, hurting yourself or others, or even possibly killing someone. I knew of a teen who was at a party and didn't drink that much, and thought he could still drive and ended up running a red light. He hit another car and severely hurt a child in the car and killed the mother. He had so much guilt that it ruined his life.

What about the risk of drinking too much and embarrassing yourself by throwing up or peeing on yourself? That sounds humiliating, right? It's because it is. It is also important to remember that drinking is illegal until you're 21; if you're underage you can get arrested. To me, it just doesn't seem worth the risks.

Another risk includes becoming addicted and needing to drink. I had a friend in high school who was addicted to alcohol; she would have to drink every morning before school and bring alcohol in her purse because she was so addicted. I remember thinking how terrible it would be to be so dependent on something that it ruled my life. If alcohol addiction runs in your family, addiction is even more likely.

Here are a few statistics regarding alcohol-related accidents.

* 60 percent of all teen deaths in car accidents are alcohol related.
* On average someone is killed in an alcohol-impaired driving crash about every 50 minutes in the U.S.
* Each year, approximately 5,000 young people under the age of 21 die as a result of underage drinking.

So, knowing the risks involved with drugs and alcohol, is it worth taking the chance? I don't think so. Just make sure you think about it and make good decisions for yourself because when you do drugs or alcohol you might not only be hurting yourself, you might be hurting someone else as well.

Just know the choice is yours...

A Teen's Journey

I was at a party and drank an entire bottle of Jack Daniel's whiskey and started throwing up and having seizures, and woke up in the hospital. I had to get my stomach pumped. It was not fun. I learned my lesson.

Think it over... and Journal

Knowing the risks involved, what do you think about alcohol? Should you be drinking, if you are?

_____

_____

_____

_____

_____

_____

_____

_____

_____

_____

_____

It's your decision to make because even though your parents may tell you not to drink, they aren't always with you. So hopefully you will make good decisions for yourself.

WHAT'S SO COOL ABOUT SMOKING?

Why do teens think it's so cool to smoke cigarettes? One big reason is that it makes them feel older and more mature, even though doing something as reckless as smoking isn't a mature thing to do. Let's talk about the risks so you can make an informed decision. Plain and simple, these are the risks of smoking cigarettes:

* Smoking kills over 400,000 people a year.
* Smoking a cigarette raises blood pressure by 5-10 mm Hg for up to 30 minutes.
* Smoking increases your risk of heart disease.
* Cigarette smoking is responsible for 151,322 cancer deaths annually in the United States. Most of those — 116,920 — are from lung cancer.
* Smoking is addictive.

Other negatives of smoking cigarettes: your breath smells like sewage; it plugs up your pores and can contribute to acne and later on to wrinkles; it can give you stomachaches; it costs a lot of money; and cigarettes are bad for the environment. What are the pros of smoking? Only that you think you look cool, but the people you look cool to are the other people who smoke.

WHAT IS VAPING?

Vaping is the inhaling of a vapor created by an electronic cigarette (e-cigarette) or other vaping device. E-cigarettes are battery-powered smoking devices. They have cartridges filled with a liquid that usually contains nicotine, flavorings, and chemicals. The liquid is heated into a vapor, which the person inhales.

WHAT ARE THE HEALTH EFFECTS OF VAPING?

Health experts are reporting serious lung damage in people who vape, including some deaths. Vaping puts nicotine into the body. Nicotine is highly addictive and can slow brain development in teens and affect memory, concentration, learning, self-control, attention, and mood. E-cigarettes also irritate the lungs, may cause serious lung damage and even death and can lead to smoking cigarettes and other forms of tobacco use.

Another scary fact is most e-cigarettes include diacetyl, a chemical that creates a buttery flavoring, in the vaping juice. When diacetyl is heated and inhaled, it causes bronchiolitis obliterans, more commonly referred to as "popcorn lung," a scarring of the tiny air sacs in the lungs resulting in a thickening and narrowing of the airways. Popcorn lung may not sound like a threat, but it's a serious lung disease that causes shortness of breath, coughing, and wheezing, symptoms similar to chronic obstructive pulmonary disease. Even though it is shown that inhaling diacetyl causes popcorn lung, this chemical can still be found in many e-cigarette flavors today.

Think it over. . . and Journal

What do you personally think the pros and cons of vaping and smoking are? If you smoke, why do you do it? If you know someone else who vapes or smokes, what do you think about it?

_____

_____

_____

_____

_____

_____

_____

_____

_____

_____

_____

When you look at the pros and cons, there aren't enough pros to make vaping or smoking okay, are there?

A Teen's Journey

A friend of mine started vaping a year ago and was complaining about his lungs hurting. It got so bad that he had to stop playing soccer. He was totally bummed. His mom took him to the Doctor's and the doctor asked him if he was vaping and told him if he didn't stop, it could do permanent damage. .

MAKING GOOD DECISIONS,
A PART OF MATURING

Learning to make good decisions for yourself is a part of growing up. Here is a quick tip list to help you become more aware of your decision-making process:

❋ When someone asks you if you want to do something, take a breath and think about it first. Weigh the pros and cons.

❋ Realize your decisions are not only affecting you, they are affecting the people around you too.

❋ Realize your decisions might affect you in the future and not just in that moment.

❋ If you state your decisions with confidence, your friends will have respect for you and probably not pressure you.

❋ Know that this is your life and you have all the power to make it what you want it to be.

Every time we make good decisions for ourselves, remember that we empower ourselves and develop a stronger sense of self. Remember the "Power Circle"— the more you do things you know are right for you, the more confidence you will have and the less you will do things that aren't good for you.

You are the only one in the driver's seat with your life. You get to make the decisions and you can't blame anyone else for how your life turns out. This is good news because I wouldn't want to put anyone else in charge of my life but me.

CHAPTER
EIGHT

Kids on the Edge—
Teen Suicide

 Why are kids committing suicide? Why do they feel there is no way out of their hopelessness? Teen suicide is the third leading cause of death for people between fifteen and twenty-four years old. It is the second leading cause of death for teens between fifteen and nineteen. Actually, only car accidents and homicides take the lives of more people between the ages of fifteen and twenty-four.

What I want to provide you with in this segment are tools. Tools for *you*, so that you can recognize if there is a problem — a problem with you or a friend — so that you can seek help before it is too late.

One of the biggest reasons for teen suicide is *depression.* Suicide usually occurs when someone is seriously upset or depressed. Teens contemplating suicide don't see any way out of problems, and they don't know how to talk to anyone about what is going on with them.

Some of the warning signs are:

❋ talking about suicide with comments like, "I won't be a problem much longer . . ."

❋ talking about feelings of hopelessness

❋ having strong feelings of guilt

❋ pulling away from friends and family

❋ not having a desire to go out and be with friends or do things

❋ experiencing changes in eating habits and sleeping habits

❋ not caring about one's appearance

❋ not thinking clearly

❋ having trouble concentrating

❋ talking about leaving or going away

❋ talking and thinking about death a lot

❋ complaining about physical pains or problems

❋ drinking a lot and/or taking drugs

❋ taking unnecessary risks

❋ not wanting to do favorite things or activities

❋ giving away possessions that are special

❋ experiencing a mood change after being depressed for a long time and then, all of a sudden, being very happy. (This could mean that a decision has been made to attempt suicide and the person is experiencing a sense of relief.)

HOW CAN WE PREVENT THESE TRAGEDIES?

It is so important to pay attention to these signs, for yourself or a friend. If you are having thoughts of suicide, talk about it. Find someone and tell them how you are feeling. Tell your parents how you feel! If you feel uncomfortable talking with your parents, go to a counselor. Go to anyone who will listen. If it is a friend, get her to talk with you about it.

A Teen's Journey

A girl at school told me she tried to kill herself when she was younger and I didn't take her seriously. I thought she was joking, and then she went home and tried to kill herself again because she didn't feel like anyone cared about her. It taught me to take it seriously when someone is talking about suicide, because you just never know.

This is why it is so important to develop self-esteem, a good sense of yourself and who you are. If you are confident and are satisfied with who you are, you are less apt to slip into a feeling of total hopelessness. When we have a strong sense of who we are, we understand that life is a process. We are here to learn from our mistakes and learn more about ourselves. Being a teen is hard. You're doing a great job. Just picking up this book is a big step toward learning how to like yourself and to learn how to be confident and satisfied with who you are.

Here is a mental health quiz. Check off any of these that describe you:

❋ I don't care about activities I used to enjoy.

❋ I don't want to be around people, not even my friends and family.

❋ I feel like I want to die.

❋ I'm using drugs and alcohol.

❋ I'm taking unnecessary risks in my life.

❋ I want to run away.

❋ I have talked about suicide.

❋ I have let my appearance go.

❋ I often have headaches, stomachaches, and other physical symptoms.

❋ I have given away some of my favorite things.

❋ My eating habits have changed.

❋ My sleeping habits have become irregular.

❋ I have difficulty concentrating.

If you have experienced three or more of these, you should seek help. Go talk to someone about how you feel. Don't let the feelings spiral out of control.

Here is the number for the National Suicide Hotline: 1-800-273-8255. A trained counselor will take your call and help you think clearly about your situation.

Here are some websites with information on teen suicide:

https://www.sprc.org

https://www.kidshealth.org

https://www.apa.org/helpcenter/teens-suicide-prevention

You are never alone. We are all connected in this life. Every action you take affects a lot of people. Reach out and get help for yourself, or help someone else who may be feeling hopeless or depressed.

Think it over. . . and Journal

If you have ever thought about suicide or you know someone who has, what are a few things you can do to get help for yourself or the other person?

_____

_____

_____

_____

_____

_____

_____

_____

_____

_____

_____

_____

Now, take the action and do them.

CHAPTER
NINE

Becoming a Woman— But I'm Still a Kid!

Your first period is the beginning of your journey to becoming a young woman. The average age for menstruation to start is twelve years old, although some girls start as early as eight or nine or as late as seventeen. Diet, exercise, and stress can play a major factor in altering your cycle. Girls who do gymnastics, take ballet, or are involved in strenuous exercise may start later. Girls with eating disorders, such as anorexia or bulimia, often do not menstruate at all.

Menstruation is when your body is preparing you for motherhood. You become fertile and are able to get pregnant. A lot of different things are happening to your body. Your hormones are changing, and your moods can fluctuate a lot during your cycle. One minute you're up and happy, and the next minute you're down and depressed. Your body is beginning to change and look more and more like a young woman. Your breasts are starting to develop. You start to get pubic and underarm hair.

The female menstrual cycle is synchronized with the cycle of the moon. The moon circles the Earth in a twenty-eight-day cycle, and most women have their menstrual cycle every twenty-eight days. Some believe that during your menstrual cycle your intuition increases. You become much more aware of things going on around you. The increase in sensitivity is like a barometer, maybe letting you know how you really feel about certain things, good or bad. Listen to it! This is a wonderful time to embrace your womanhood.

When I was younger I remember things happening about three days before and during my period that I didn't pay much attention to. My hearing became so acute that I could hear things I normally couldn't hear. Also if music was too loud it would hurt my ears. I also remember being very sensitive to my feelings, and more emotionally responsive. What I came to realize with age was that my intuition was really kicking in and talking to me. The sensitivity was my body trying to tell me something, maybe that something was off in my life and to look at it. An example of this is I had a guy friend who wasn't that great of a friend to me. I kept the friendship going even though we weren't that close. Every month during my cycle when this friend and I would get together, it was almost like my insides were screaming out "Why are you friends with this guy?" The voice became so loud that I couldn't ignore it any longer. So I finally decided to end the friendship. It changed my life to release him. Once I released his friendship, I opened up a gate for more available male friends to come in. I now have good male friendships in my life. So pay attention to what your body is saying to you during your cycle. It could change your life. It is a very special process that women get to experience every month.

We have been conditioned to view this time as a negative monthly event in our lives when it is actually a very special time. This time of the month does not have to be a bad thing if you embrace it. Embrace your womanhood and love how you feel! Love your emotions, your extra

sensitivity, and increased intuition. Realize what a beautiful gift it is to be a woman and to be able to bear children some day — *after you are an adult.*

Unfortunately, I have seen many of us take this beautiful experience every month and turn it into some horrible thing. What do we call it? "The curse." Oh my, that sounds evil. "The rag." That sounds dirty. "My period." That's not as bad, although it sounds like the end of something. How about naming it something that sounds positive? "My moon." The moon is big, bright, and powerful. Women are bright and powerful too.

Both of my daughters have suffered with bad cramps during their "moons." When they started to embrace these times of the month and be all right with all that goes with it, their cramping seemed to decrease. This is a wonderful time to experience the feelings of being a woman. I would suggest reading up on exactly what happens to your body when you are having your "moon." Then as you understand it more, you can embrace the real beauty in it. A good website to view on what happens to your body before and during your "moon" is: www.kidshealth.org.

Think it over. . . and Journal

Write down your feelings about your moon (menstruation). If they are negative feelings, write down some of the positive aspects you remember from this chapter.

_____

_____

_____

_____

_____

_____

_____

_____

_____

_____

_____

_____

Remember how lucky we are to be women and all the positive things that go along with our moons.

CHAPTER
TEN

Sex! Is There a Price to Pay?

 Is there a price to pay?? YES!!! Pregnancy or getting a sexually transmitted disease (STD), having to tell the man you love and want to marry that you have had many sexual partners, that you have a sexually transmitted disease that he is going to get, and that you'll both have it for the rest of your lives! And then there's living with an STD. *Absolutely* there is a price to pay. Sexuality is big! It is such an important link to our self-esteem.

Sex is such a wonderful gift we both give to and receive from a person that we trust with every fiber of our being. It should never be treated casually. When the gift is exchanged with someone we don't know, who is to say if they will care about the gift and treat it with respect?

When we have sex with another person, we are physically and emotionally as close as two people can be. Why would we want to be that close to someone we don't know well?

Would you take your clothes off in front of a complete stranger? Of course not. EXACTLY!

I was talking to a girl who told me she was seeing this guy and he

was really coming on strong and wanting her to have sex with him. He was telling her that he loved her and that he could picture them together forever. She liked him a lot. She really wanted him to keep liking her, so she finally had sex with him. The next day in school he barely talked to her, and his friends would laugh when she walked by. She felt so stupid and hurt. She wanted to drop out of school she felt so bad. But she learned a good lesson. This girl never had sex with anyone again until she was totally sure about the relationship and how she really felt about the guy. She actually ended up waiting several years and never regretted her decision.

When we have casual sex, it leaves us feeling empty and cold. Our self-esteem takes a beating, leaving it lying in the middle of the road, just waiting for a truck to run it over.

When we treat sex in a casual way, our self-esteem is most vulnerable. Having sex to get someone to like you or to stay with you never works and will leave you emotionally torn into pieces. You don't need to get anyone to like you or to accept you if you like yourself. And if it takes sex to keep a boyfriend, he isn't worth having. Let him go!

First of all, having sex with someone will not make him like or accept you. Maybe it will make him want to be with you more often, but it will be only for more sex. I don't know about you, but I want someone to want to be with me because he likes, respects, and *wants* to be with me, not just because he wants to have sex. If a guy really likes you, he will respect you and your decision not to have sex. If you really want to find out if your boyfriend really likes you, that is the way. If he does, he will want to be your boyfriend even if means not having sex. Maybe you will even find a guy who has respect for himself and wants to wait until he's more mature. He may not want to have sex casually. This kind of guy knows that having sex doesn't make him a man. A man is someone who has respect for himself and girls.

Being a guy is tough sexually, because other guys expect you to be a certain way. For me, I strongly disagree with having casual sex because sex should be sacred and should be shared between two people that are in love and mature enough to handle everything that comes with it.

The best system is to get to know a guy really well before becoming his girlfriend. When you meet a guy, why not become good friends with him first? Get to know him; find out what he likes and doesn't like. See if you're compatible. If you're friends for awhile, and he isn't your type, the worst-case scenario is that you have a good friend. Diving right into a relationship with a guy without knowing him gets your emotions involved and a little out of whack. When your emotions are involved, you don't see clearly. You might not make good decisions for yourself, like having sex with someone who really doesn't care about you.

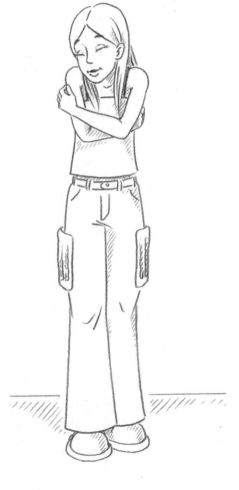

I know it's hard sometimes to be the only one in your group of friends without a boyfriend, but think about how much better it is going to be in the long run. If one of your girlfriends is upset like my girlfriend was, and is feeling humiliated about a guy leaving her after having sex with her, you are in a place where you can give her advice. You can explain to her that you avoid that kind of situation completely by starting with a friendship first.

Boys want to have sex! A lot of boys will do and say anything to have it. Girls want to be loved, and many girls will have sex mistakenly thinking that they will get the love they want. This is why it is so important to love yourself so that you will not be willing to have sex to get love that you lack for yourself.

Loving yourself means having self-esteem, and having self-esteem will help you to avoid making mistakes.

Another important thing to think about is what may happen if you have sex. One day I was sitting outside with my oldest daughter and two of her closest friends. They were all thirteen years old at the time. We were talking about boys and sex, and I looked at all of them and said, "Let's say you're pregnant. What are you going to do?" They all became very quiet, and I could tell they were thinking very hard. I first asked my daughter. She said, "Have the baby and give it to a good home." I then looked at the next girl. She said "Have an abortion." Then the last friend said, "Have the baby and keep it." I was amazed that three very close girlfriends had three very different solutions to the same problem. We started to talk about what all of these options really meant.

It is true that if you have sex, you can get pregnant. It is as simple as that. It's a good idea to think about it and consider what that might mean to you. I'm sure there are girls of all ages at your school dealing with this very problem.

What I'm going to say now is pretty straightforward, and I apologize if it sounds harsh, but the reality is that if you are pregnant, choosing any one of these options is going to be very difficult. One of them might be better for you and for the baby, but unfortunately, none of them will be easy.

So let's look at the first option: having the baby and giving the baby up for adoption. Being pregnant puts your body through a lot, especially a young body that's not quite ready for childbirth. Imagine being pregnant in school or having to drop out. Really picture that! Then think about giving your baby to someone you probably don't even know. Fortunately, there are a lot of couples who want babies, and they may be better prepared emotionally and financially to care for a child. So that is one option.

The next difficult option is to have an abortion. An abortion is when a doctor terminates your pregnancy. It is a medical procedure, done in a hospital, which removes the fetus from your body. The doctor takes a sterile medical vacuum and literally sucks the fetus out. The physical recovery time is minimal, but the emotional recovery may take years. Think about all areas of healing: physical, mental, and emotional. This is the second option.

Now let's look at the last option available. This would be having the baby and raising it yourself. If you're thirteen years old, you're just a kid. Your body is not fully matured yet. Even though you can get pregnant, it's truly quite young to be carrying and delivering a baby. How about raising a baby when you're thirteen years old, or even fourteen, fifteen, or sixteen? While you're at home changing diapers, your friends are still in school and having fun. They are going to dances and having sleepovers, and you're at home putting your baby to bed. While you are working to finish school, you will also have the immense responsibility of raising your child. Taking care of a baby day in and day out is really tough. You're up during the nights and right back at it in the morning. This baby isn't a doll you can put away when you're bored with it. It is a lifetime commitment. The baby depends on you for everything: for the food she eats, for her shelter, for her health care, and especially, for a lot of love and affection.

I remember telling my girls that if they ever got pregnant and decided to keep the baby, that they would be the mom, not me. When you have a baby, *you* are the mother and no one else. That means that the baby looks to *you* for everything. When your friends are getting together to have fun, there is more than a good possibility that you would be staying home with your baby and being a mom instead.

All right, those are the options, OH WAIT! I just thought of another option. DON'T HAVE SEX UNTIL YOU'RE OLD ENOUGH AND MATURE ENOUGH AND CAN AFFORD TO BE A MOM!!!!!!!!!!!!

The bottom line is that all of these options are challenging. If you are pregnant and looking at the options, one of them will work for you. I suggest talking to someone who can help you through the process of making this difficult decision. If you are *not* pregnant, realize what the consequences of having sex are. Really think about it!

So, do you think getting pregnant is the worst thing that can happen to you if you have sex? Pregnancy has its solutions.

SEXUALLY TRANSMITTED INFECTIONS

Sexually transmitted infections (STIs) are diseases that can be transmitted to another person during sexual activity. This activity is not just sexual intercourse. STIs can be given to another person through an exchange of bodily fluids, secretions, or genital contact. And there are a multitude of them! Some of them aren't curable, which means you will have them for the rest of your life. Some of them even cause death. Some STIs, like chlamydia, may prevent you from having children after you are married and really want children.

So if you still decide to have sex, you at least know that there are huge risks involved, and it isn't worth the risk to have sex with some guy you barely know. *Trust me!* Condoms don't always protect against pregnancy or STIs. And you just may be right back at the other options for getting pregnant even if you do use protection! The only way to avoid getting pregnant and to be 100 percent sure is *not* to have SEX! The only way to avoid getting a sexually transmitted disease is not to have SEX!

It is your responsibility to make sure you are doing what is in your best interest. You must take the responsibility of your actions for you *will* experience their results. Don't be embarrassed to talk to your mom or a counselor or maybe an older sister or aunt. One of them may be able to help you think about these things and answer questions.

Here is a good website about STIs: https://www.cdc.gov/std/. Having sex before you're mature enough to know the serious issues involved can cause both emotional and physical damage. Sorry to get so heavy, but having sex before you are aware of *all* the consequences is truly serious.

Having sexual relationships with someone whom you don't know or trust can be very damaging to your emotional body as well as your physical body. Take care of yourself, don't treat yourself with such casualness. Get to know a guy before becoming his girlfriend. Most of the time girls just jump into relationships with guys before they know who they are.

I had a client who met this guy and six months later they were married. Two months later he came home after having a beer with some friends and picked a fight with her. No matter what she said, it made him angrier. He started to hit her and didn't stop until she was pretty beat up. He apologized and said he would never do it again. Well, two weeks later it happened again, but this time he put her in the hospital. She called me at 2:00 a.m.; I was shocked, but should I have been? She really didn't even know him. He treated her really well in the beginning and because of her lack of love for herself, he filled a big hole in her. After she left the hospital she came to me, and we did a lot of talking about how she felt about herself. She admitted to having a low sense of herself. She realized that she went into the relationship without knowing the man. She brought him into her home and into her heart. He wasn't a safe person to bring in.

But, how do we know if he is safe? We *don't* unless we take the time to get to know him. Eventually he will show who he is. He will only be able to pretend for so long; if he has behavior that isn't good, it will come out, even as a friend. The worst thing that can happen is you spend eight months or so getting to know him. If within that eight months he turns out to be a jerk, you walk away without any emotional ties. Or he is an okay guy, just not your type, you end up with a good friend. Or he is a great guy and he is your type and you both like each other enough to take it to the next level. If we don't get to know someone it's like holding our heart out in the palm of our hand; if it's a safe person, lucky you, if it's not, it feels like he grabs your heart, throws it on the ground, and stomps on it. No thank you! It makes more sense to get to know someone first. I believe that when we love ourselves we don't look outside of ourselves for that love. If someone comes into your life and treats you like a princess, it's nice, but don't fall head over heels in love. Think it's nice, but stand back, wait to get to know him and see what the real picture is.

Sex has become very casual in today's world and unfortunately some girls think it's cool to sleep around. I believe this is going to affect them in their adult years. Even if other girls are having casual sex, you don't have to.

WHAT MAKES A GIRL PRETTY, IN A GUY'S EYES?

Here are some comments from junior high and high school guys about what makes a girl pretty. I think these comments will surprise you. There are guys out there who care about other things beside looks, you just have to find them and say no to those other guys who only care about how you look on the outside.

Here are some comments on what makes a girl pretty from some very special guys.

❀ That she is smart and funny with good morals.

❀ A good personality, smile, and laugh.

❀ What's on the inside makes a girl pretty.

❀ What really makes a girl pretty is how she acts and her personality, and how she treats people who aren't her friends.

❀ What kind of a person she is, because it won't matter how cute she is if she is a mean person.

❀ If her personality is bad it doesn't matter how pretty she is, in my eyes she isn't. There is this girl that everyone thinks is so pretty but she is so mean and she has such a bad attitude, so I just don't see it.

❀ A great personality and fun to be around.

❀ Her ability to laugh with me, that's the most important thing.

❀ What makes a girl pretty to me is a lot of good qualities like she's nice to people and she is honest.

❀ Girls that are humble about their looks. There is nothing worse than a pretty girl who knows it.

❋ I think smart girls are pretty to me.

❋ What makes a girl beautiful is her sense of herself, her confidence.

❋ If she is real, being herself, not trying to be perfect.

❋ A girl that doesn't wear a lot of makeup, that's more natural.

❋ A girl that loves and respects herself.

❋ A personality that you can enjoy and really connect to, because over time looks go away but your personality is always going to affect the relationship.

❋ She has to be beautiful inside and be nice to everyone.

When I was visiting the schools gathering this information, I shared some of these comments with the girls and they were shocked that there were guys who felt this way. There are good guys out there. It's your job to find them and not be in relationships with guys who only want you because of your looks or to have sex with you.

CHAPTER
ELEVEN

Have You Started the Healing Yet?

 As you look back at all the chapters in this book, you can see that our main goal has been to achieve self-esteem and to heal in all areas of our life so that we are confident and satisfied with ourselves.

Learning to like yourself is key. Make sure you are doing things in your life that promote self-acceptance like:

* Treating people in ways you would like to be treated
* Not judging others, accepting them for who they are
* Making decisions knowing that you are not the only one affected
* Having integrity
* Finishing projects
* Taking care of yourself physically and spiritually
* Managing your negative voice
* Being in relationships with people who treat you right and are honest with you
* Looking to yourself for acceptance, not others
* Having respect for yourself sexually

❋ Not numbing yourself with drugs

❋ Embracing your womanhood

❋ Taking responsibility for your actions

❋ Walking through your fears

❋ Creating, giving everything a chance

❋ Being there 100 percent

❋ Realizing you play an important part in the world

If you do things that ensure self-acceptance, your self-esteem will have room to grow. It is also important to realize that if you face your fears, they have no power over you. Your fears only have the power you give them. If you are afraid of something, look at it and decide if it is a valid fear or if it's something that's holding you back from really living.

For me, talking in front of people is a fear that I am working on all the time. But every time I get up in front of a crowd and speak, it actually feels a lot better. I no longer shake and get sick to my stomach. The more I walk through that fear, the less hold it has on me. Now every time I speak in front of people I feel good about myself. This good feeling promotes confidence and satisfaction. Remember, satisfaction + confidence in oneself = self-esteem.

The way to heal insecure feelings about your creativity is simply to create. Give all creations a chance. Do a hobby long enough to develop your skills. Try a lot of different things to see which one feels good to you.

A good way to heal your physical health is to start taking action. If you are feeding your body bad food, then stop! If you are vaping, stop! Start an exercise program; any small start will do. Start treating your body with care and be good to it. It is the only vehicle you've been given to take

you around this life. If you're not caring for your skin, start a program. Keep your stress in check and get enough sleep. If you are suffering with an eating disorder, seek help. Know that you are special and unique and deserve to be happy.

As far as your spiritual health goes . . . well, you already have started to take action by reading this book. Keep evolving and growing. Hang around with friends who are real with you instead of just saying and doing what they think you want them to say and do. Let them be a mirror for you. Realize that we are all teachers at certain times and students at others, and that we truly make a difference in people's lives. Everything we say and do affects the world.

If you are doing drugs, ask yourself why. Really take a look at why and stop being destructive to your physical and emotional body. Being present to experience this amazing life is powerful. It can't be done if you are numb.

If even the smallest thought about suicide has entered your head, seek help. Talk to someone. You are an important part of the world. Start looking at yourself and start to accept yourself for the beautiful person you are and the beautiful person you are becoming.

Stop blaming people for things that happen in your life. Realize that your parents are people too. No matter how they act, they are people who love you and are doing the best they can do. Let them have room to grow too. They might make mistakes. They are not perfect, and that is okay. Love them for the journey they are on and for how hard they are working to do what is right for you.

Embrace your womanhood. It is a beautiful gift you have been given. Women are special spirits with intuition and power that cannot be denied.

A good way to heal yourself sexually is to respect and love yourself. Do not have sex for the wrong reasons. Really think about what is at risk, and what price you might have to pay. It's not just *your* life that is at stake, but maybe a little baby's life too.

Everything we have talked about is wrapped up with your self-esteem. Everything you do affects your self-esteem.

How you experience everything in life comes down to whether or not you have cultivated self-esteem. And just what can you do to have this confidence and this sense of satisfaction? Every time you feel bad, it is because you haven't developed your strengths in a certain area. Look at yourself. Pay attention to yourself and to everything around you. Know that you are an important part of the universe and that you affect everyone in it. Use what you see and what you learn to love yourself and to make the best decisions about your life.

Everything we've talked about will point you in the direction of becoming what you dream of: a powerful young woman. The only way to become a powerful woman, with the brilliance of a shining star, is to have a strong sense of who you are.

❋ Accept the things you can't change about yourself and love yourself anyway.

❋ Change the things about yourself that you can change.

❋ Stop blaming everyone for who you are or circumstances you are in.

❋ Do things that keep your physical body healthy, so that you have the energy to make the changes in your life that you want.

❋ Challenge yourself constantly to grow and develop self-pride.

❋ Take action in your life. You can't heal yourself without taking action!

❋ Stop talking about the things you want to do and just do them!

❋ Realize that your actions affect a lot of people. Be kind, but be real.

❋ Walk through the things that scare you.

❋ Don't let the opinions of others about you affect your happiness or make you sad.

❋ Know that being a woman is special.

❋ Treat your sexuality with the respect it deserves.

❋ Be present, be here!

❋ Just be yourself.

You already have the power within yourself. Use it! You are strong enough to take care of yourself. The more you care for yourself, the stronger you will become. Just take action, and do it! Become a person who is confident and satisfied with herself.

Journaling Notes

_____

_____

_____

_____

_____

_____

_____

_____

_____

_____

_____

_____

_____

_____

_____

Journaling Notes

_____

_____

_____

_____

_____

_____

_____

_____

_____

_____

_____

_____

_____

_____

_____

_____

Journaling Notes

_____

_____

_____

_____

_____

_____

_____

_____

_____

_____

_____

_____

_____

_____

_____

_____

Journaling Notes

Journaling Notes

_____

_____

_____

_____

_____

_____

_____

_____

_____

_____

_____

_____

_____

_____

_____

Journaling Notes

_____

_____

_____

_____

_____

_____

_____

_____

_____

_____

_____

_____

_____

_____

Resources from Debra

Hello teens and parents. I just want to emphasize how committed I am to helping you through these turbulent years. I hope to give you both all the tools you need, so here is a list of resources for you that I have found to be helpful. This can be a tricky time for both teens and parents, and the more resources you have the better you will be able to cope with all of the circumstances. Remember that I mentor both teens and parents face-to-face, or by phone. I also do Mother/Daughter Breakthrough Retreats in Sedona, which are very empowering.

My heart is with you whether you are a teenage girl or a parent. My goal is to help both of you navigate through these confusing times with more love and understanding for yourself and each other. Hopefully, teens, *My Feet Aren't Ugly* is a powerful tool to help you learn more about what it means to truly love yourself and take the action necessary to create the life you want. Parents, I am currently working on a parenting book that will help you develop the tools you need to be a strong parent while supporting your teen through your heart.

www.EmpoweredTeensandParents.com
Debra@EmpoweredTeensandParents.com
Like Empowered Teens and Parents on Facebook
www.SedonaSoulRetrieval.com (Adult Retreats and Mentoring)
Debra@SedonaSoulRetrieval.com

Other Helpful Resources

Girlshealth.gov

Teenoverthecounterdrugabuse.com

Stopcyberbullying.com

Teen Suicide Kidshealth.org

Teen smoking Cdc.gov

National Highway Traffic Safety and Administration nhtsa.gov